Praise for
DAD *Spelled Backward*

"M. S. King's *Dad Spelled Backward* chronicles his and his wife's frustrating yet fulfilling quest to have a baby. King, a New York dentist and comedian, was in his fifties when he met Gaby. When King was younger, his Jewish mother had hoped he would marry a woman of the same faith, but, King notes, the passage of time had rendered his mother happy that he had just found a 'mammal' to marry. She was delighted by his intelligent, beautiful French bride.

"Though King was undecided about having children, Gaby was determined to get pregnant. The couple's initial conception attempts, or what King calls "Fertility Hell," involved familiar procedures, like filling sperm-specimen cups and obsessive tracking of Gaby's ovulation cycles. King also tried natural 'virility enhancers' such as yohimbe and ginseng; he ended up in the hospital when their combined effect began to feel like a heart attack. Later, a Chinese acupuncturist advised King to "drink more water" for his weak kidneys, while positioning needles throughout his body to stimulate potency and 'chi.'

"After further fertility tests and unsuccessful artificial insemination, King and Gaby decided to adopt. *Dad Spelled Backward* recounts the arduous process that followed, including posting adoption advertisements, interviewing respondents, and their feelings of intense disappointment after a birth mother opted to keep her baby. The couple's costs ran high: there were attorney and administrative fees, as well as plane fares to meet with prospective candidates. There was also the psychological toll of prolonged expectation.

"*Dad Spelled Backward* is a heartfelt, sage, and funny look at the worthwhile gauntlet of domestic adoption. It's also a compelling portrait of a marriage, showing how the bond between King and his wife grew stronger and more resilient as they navigated their unique path to parenthood."

—ForeWord Reviews

DAD

SPELLED BACKWARD

A Journey Through the Maze of
Love, Marriage, and Adoption

By M. S. King

Cypress House
Fort Bragg, California

Publisher's Cataloging-in-Publication
(Provided by Cassidy Cataloguing Services, Inc.)

Names: King, M. S. (Michael S.), 1950- author.
Title: Dad spelled backward : a journey through the maze of love,
    marriage, and adoption / by M.S. King.
Description: First edition. | Fort Bragg, California : Cypress House, [2022]
Identifiers: ISBN: 979-8-9854086-0-7 (paperback) | 979-8-9854086-1-4 (ePub) |
    LCCN: 2022937138
Subjects: LCSH: Married people--Humor. | Fatherhood--Humor. | Infertility--
    Treatment--Humor. | Intercountry adoption--Humor. | Dentists--New
    York (State)--New York--Humor. | LCGFT: Humor. | BISAC: HEALTH
    & FITNESS / Fertility & Infertility. | HUMOR / Topic / Marriage &
    Family.
    Classification: LCC: HQ734 .K56 2022 | DDC: 306.81--dc23

Library of Congress Control Number: 2022937138

ISBN: 979-8-9854086-0-7
epub ISBN: 979-8-9854086-1-4

First Edition
10 9 8 7 6 5 4 3 2 1

For my extraordinary family

Contents

THIS BOOK EXPLORES the journey my wife and I undertook on the road to becoming parents. It describes *our* journey. Your mileage may vary. There is absolutely no assurance or warranty that any statement contained or cited in this book is true, correct, precise, or up to date. Even if a statement is accurate, it may not apply to you or your situation. You are encouraged to confirm any information obtained from or through this book with other sources.

The medical information provided in this book is, at best, of a general nature and cannot substitute for the advice of a medical professional. I do not recommend, endorse, or make any representation about the efficacy, appropriateness, or suitability of any specific tests, products, procedures, treatments, services, opinions, health-care providers, or other information contained in this book.

Also included in this book is information on the various laws regarding adoption that we encountered. This book is not intended or implied to be a substitute for professional legal guidance.

Neither author nor publisher are responsible nor liable for any advice, course of treatment, diagnosis, or any other information that you obtain (or think you have obtained) through this book.

Part I
Peter Pan

CHAPTER I

Tick-Tock

CAN YOU DIE FROM HAVING TOO MUCH SEX? I wondered. My much younger wife and I were having a lot of sex lately, more so than usual. I was dog-tired exhausted. But I don't want to get ahead of myself. It was a Saturday afternoon. Gaby was doing some shopping, and I was resting and waiting for her at a Starbucks on the Upper West Side. As I sat and drank my chai latte, I looked over the diverse crowd.

A diminutive blond mom walked through the entrance. She appeared stressed out, struggling to hold her baby while pushing another child, a toddler, in a sleek Bugaboo stroller.

"Did you poop, Jordan?" she asked. Jordan was silent in her arms, so the mom lifted him and put her nose to his butt. From her expression, Jordan had made a poop, and a smelly one at that. "Jordan, we had a deal. You're supposed to tell Mommy when you go potty."

Apparently, Jordan hadn't gotten the "poop in my pants" memo. And if he had, what sound would an as-yet-unable-to-speak child make to convey the word "poop"?

I'm not ready for that!

The idea of changing a baby's poop-smeared diaper disgusted me: not just smelling it, but seeing it, cleaning it off the baby's bum. Hell, just thinking about it made me want to vomit. And it had to get on your hands sometimes, right? Touching another human being's poop, even a baby's, was out of the question.

"You'll do anything for your kid, and changing their shit-filled diaper is the least of it," my dear friend Richard told me over the phone later as I related my Starbucks experience to him. "They could shit on your head and you wouldn't care."

"I couldn't do it," I told him. "I'd let their diaper explode before I'd change it."

Maybe this was why Richard and Sandra had never asked me to babysit.

"You say that now," Richard said. "But you'll see. Once you have that kid, everything fucking changes."

"It doesn't have to change, right?" I asked. "I mean, you still can keep doing some of the things you've been doing?"

"You're a fucking idiot," Richard said. "You used to be my idol. Living the life. Single with money. You had great stories about women. And then you got married. Fine, Gabriella is great. I love her. But having kids, that is a whole other thing. They're like little vampires who suck the life out of you. Your life belongs to them. I haven't done what I want in seventeen years. Do you really want a fucking kid?"

I didn't know how to answer that. It was an easy question to ask once you already had a kid. It reminded me of people with money who say they would be just as happy without it—we all know that's bullshit. Richard would be miserable without his kids.

Gaby and I barely talked about it. We talked about being able to travel the world. We talked about one day spending some time in Bali, the trip of a lifetime, on some special future occasion.

I didn't envision that trip with a child. Then again, we weren't using any form of birth control, so the possibility of getting pregnant was there. And what was with all the sex lately? Was she trying to tell me something? We both liked kids, but having them just didn't seem to be a hot topic of conversation. Part of me thought if it was meant to be, it would happen when the time was right. Somehow nature would take care of us. I thought Gaby felt the same; if not, wouldn't she have said something?

Sure, I'm getting old. But I still have time. Aren't people, especially in Manhattan, having children later and later in life or not having kids at all? Why not us?

I was fine with the status quo. Why rock the boat? Happy couple, happy life without kids. What was that old Doris Day song, *Que Será, Será*—whatever will be, will be? Life was great and I didn't need a baby to complicate things.

And then that all changed.

CHAPTER 2

Sex Fiend?

WE WERE HAVING DINNER AT A CHARMING TURKISH restaurant in our neighborhood. I was dunking warm pita bread into a creamy hummus when Gaby brought up the subject.

"Do you think maybe we can't get pregnant?" It was the first time she had addressed the issue with so much directness. I almost choked on the pita.

I knew things were about to change. Gaby was no longer on the fence about having kids and satisfied with waiting. She wanted to get pregnant.

"There's nothing wrong," I said. "Sometimes these things just take time."

"I know, but we haven't been taking any precautions for nearly a year and nothing has happened," Gaby said. "You know I'm pushing forty."

"We've got time," I said, but knew it was a lie. "I'm barely fifty-four, and you could pass for a college coed."

"You Americans are so obsessed with staying young," Gaby said. "Stop it—my inside clock is not waiting for you to make up your mind."

It's "biological clock," sweetheart.

She was right about that. I was obsessed with staying young, and having a kid was so grown-up and responsible. What was it called, the Peter Pan syndrome? I was barely used to being married, and now the kid conversation was real and upon us in earnest. It seemed too fast. A kid would change everything. And wouldn't Gaby spend more time with the kid than with me? Nothing would be the same. Kids drooled all over the place. Disgusting. You didn't get any sleep when you had a kid. I needed my sleep. And all the kid-crap would be lying all over the place. I could trip on a toy and break my neck. *Who needs that shit? I don't.*

I was so conflicted. I knew the age thing was just an excuse, an easy way out for not having a child. I was in great shape, probably better shape than a lot of thirty-year-olds. I could easily handle taking care of a child. It went much deeper than that. Yes, I wanted to make my wife happy, but I didn't want to make my life miserable. The stress and responsibility of a child would do that to me. I thought I'd feel different if we waited. I needed time to sort things out, to adjust to the idea of having a child. With time, maybe I'd be on board, ready for that baby in our life. Ready to make the commitment. *Shit, but Gaby wants a baby now.*

Why hadn't she talked about it sooner? Was she just trying to make me happy by waiting, knowing that was what I wanted? How could I not see that? How could I have been so selfish?

I was out of time. No more bullshit excuses or delays. My wife wanted a baby. She wanted a family. She deserved a family. I loved her so much and needed to make her happy. What the fuck was I going to do?

Maybe it was just a phase she was going through and it would all go away.

Who am I fucking kidding?

It seemed so true, that cliché: happy wife, happy life. I realized that in order for that to work, I had to keep certain things in my mind. *We don't need a fucking kid, honey,* was not an option. It would make her miserable and in turn make my life miserable. Do husbands internalize for preservation? Absolutely! We want to live. Is surrender one of the keys to a successful marriage? Totally! There was no getting around it. My wife wanted a baby . . . NOW!

"Look at these, please," Gaby said a few weeks later as she plopped a few books, maybe twenty, onto my desk. I stopped to look at the pile. All of them were about one thing: getting pregnant. I had already looked at the multiple Internet sites Gaby had told me about, as well as the many instructional videos on YouTube about how to increase our chances of getting pregnant. Add to that the advice and tips from friends, and it seemed like everyone was an expert when it came to getting pregnant.

The number-one simplest bit of advice for getting pregnant seemed to be this: just do it. Do it as much as you can.

Richard summed it up best. "Just do it every day, twice a day, every hour if needed. Don't even think about it. Just do it all the time."

"We're already doing it all the time," I said. "How can we do it more? I don't think I can."

"Think rabbit," Richard said. "You're a giant, horny, humping, fucking rabbit. Rabbits . . . just fuck, fuck, and fuck."

We did it more often and everywhere: in the kitchen, on the floor, in the car, in the bathroom of a friend's house, on the beach, on a hike, in a movie theater, while she was on the phone with her parents. It was sick!

We would think of new places and new ways to do it. "How about at my office on the dental chair?" I suggested. "We can even use a little laughing gas." And so we fucked laughing.

"How about in my office—or better yet, in my boss's office, under her desk?" Gaby suggested.

"How naughty," I agreed. So one night after work we went there and went at it, right under the boss's desk.

"What was that?" I said, stopping abruptly. "Did you hear that?"

"It's just John, the janitor," Gaby said. "We're okay. This is the last room he cleans. We've still got twenty minutes before he comes in here."

Concerned, I thought about it for a moment. "Oh, okay." We continued and crossed the boss's office off our list.

My exhaustion got worse. I started taking natural over-the-counter stimulants to combat my sex fatigue, like ginseng and stay-awake pills. Still, as life often teaches us, too much of a good thing can grow stale. We began to lose our spontaneity. We needed to find new turn-ons because simple stories and diverse locations were no longer good enough for us. We had to travel to the world of kink. First, we'd dress up. You know, nurse and doctor, or in our case, hygienist and dentist.

"Does the doctor want to drill me tonight?" Gaby asked, wearing a lab coat with nothing underneath.

Our stories got wilder, more inventive. The naughtier the story, the better it worked for me. It was like psychological Viagra. But as with any drug, after a while you needed more to get high.

Porn: such a little word that says so much. We tried that, too. And with the Internet, you didn't have to feel like a creep while looking at the porn selection in the back of the neighborhood kiosk. You could feel like a creep without ever leaving your home. We each had our favorites. I liked plotless, gratuitous porn. Gaby was partial to porn with more of a story line.

At the center of it all was the ever-important menstrual cycle. The medical literature we read confused me as to when it was best to have sex if we wanted to get pregnant. It said it was best to have sex within a day or two of ovulation, which is usually about fourteen days after a woman's last period. But ovulation time can vary from cycle to cycle, and then you had to factor in how long the egg lives, usually twelve to twenty-four hours. That left a window of opportunity of only a few days, but since we were having sex all time, we figured the odds were good that we'd get it done.

Having the sex was the easy part; it was the waiting that was hard—waiting for her period to begin or not. With each succeeding month we tried, Gaby's menstrual cycle became more important. A day or two late and we'd get out the early pregnancy tests and hold our breath as we looked for a change in color on the stick. Negative, negative, negative. Maybe it was the pregnancy test itself? We tried every brand, multiple times each month. Negative, negative, negative!

Nothing was happening. I blamed myself. It wasn't Gaby. She was much younger; her eggs had to be good. It had to be my lazy old sperm. Sure, there were millions and millions of them, but not enough, I reasoned. I needed billions. My balls needed to work overtime so that her little egg wouldn't stand a chance against my army of invaders. Woody Allen played a sperm in the movie *Everything You Always Wanted to Know About Sex* But Were Afraid to Ask*. I needed one like him, just one cunning soldier to get through the enemy line.

Without telling Gaby, I started buying other products to increase my sperm count. And there were a lot of them out there.

"Can't get her pregnant? Well, Penis Power is for you."

"Sperm Flow Extract, guaranteed to increase your testosterone and sperm count with just one pill."

I took dietary supplements as well, like selenium, zinc, vitamin E, and many others that supposedly helped boost my count.

I wanted to become a sexual machine—the most virile man alive. Sperm-Man was here to save the day and get us pregnant.

In addition, I followed other Internet advice that would assure my swimmers were operating at peak efficiency.

Wear loose underwear. (Apparently loose balls are more productive than tight ones.)

Avoid hot baths and showers. (Sperm work better when cooled like champagne.)

Avoid putting your cellphone in your front pocket. (Sperm aren't fond of the electromagnetic radiation emitted by cellphones.)

Be careful never, ever to take a hot bath with your cellphone near your testicles.

And then there were the virility enhancers like yohimbe, horny goat weed (seriously?), and other strange herbal formulas with names I could barely pronounce. My penis was the gun and my sperm the bullets; virility enhancers were the extra gunpowder that would give the biggest bang, so to speak.

I started popping the pills more often: in the morning; after I got home from work. At first it seemed like things were buzzing along.

Gaby seemed delighted that her man was performing like a sex addict . . . although she thought I seemed a little hyper. I was a bit edgy, perhaps, but it was a small price to pay for prowess in bed.

Everything seemed fine, except I started noticing some changes. I found myself doing dental fillings in half the time while jabbering to my dental assistant and patient the whole time I was drilling.

I would eat my meals in about three gulps. At staff meetings it seemed like I couldn't get the words out fast enough to keep up with my thoughts. My office manager, Rachel, asked me if I was on something. "Coffee," I explained. "I've just been drinking more coffee."

I'd stay up till the wee hours of the morning doing chores. Sometimes I couldn't sleep and would go jogging around the streets of New York City at two a.m. Then when I got home, I'd scrub the kitchen floor. It was NoDoz to the tenth power. I felt like the Road Runner. The pills were affecting my life not only in the bedroom but in general.

One Tuesday night we were at a trendy restaurant in the West Village. Dining out on a Tuesday worked well for people who didn't care about being "in." It was less crowded and allowed us to enjoy good food with conversations we could hear.

I was sipping an Argentinean Malbec when I felt a sudden pounding in my chest. I could actually feel the rapid beat of my heart against my chest wall. "One, two, three, four." I could hear the beats bouncing around in my head. It was like an alien was trying to get out.

"I think I'm having a heart attack," I said, putting my wine down.

"What do you mean?" Gaby asked.

"A heart attack. You know when you grab your chest, keel over, and die?" I said, noticing that she didn't even look up from her food. I went back to my oysters.

"You're not grabbing your chest," Gaby said, now looking at me.

"I'm still eating," I said. I was halfway through a plate of two dozen oysters. (I'd heard that oysters were supposed to be an aphrodisiac even though Richard had so kindly informed me, "That's just a fucking myth thrown out there by oyster fishermen.")

"If you still care about food, you're not having a heart attack," Gaby said.

"Here, feel." I took Gaby's hand and put it over my heart. "Feel that."

"Your heart is beating. That's very good."

"But it shouldn't beat that fast." I looked at my watch.

"It's probably just indigestion, Michael. You always eat too fast."

"Shush. I'm counting my heartbeats. Twenty in ten seconds. That's a hundred twenty in a minute. Isn't that a lot?"

"How many beats are we supposed to have per minute?" Gaby asked.

"I'm not positive—I think around seventy."

"You're the doctor. Shouldn't you know that?"

"You forget when it's your own heart."

All those science courses I took in dental school seemed to vanish in the throes of death.

"Can you Google it?" I asked.

"Now?" Gaby replied. "You're not the only one still eating."

"Well, if seventy is normal, a hundred twenty can't be good."

"I think you overdid it with the oysters," Gaby said. "That many will give anyone indigestion. Here, try my salmon." She scooped up a piece of fish and put it in front of my mouth. I ate it.

"That's really good. Try an oyster." I placed a slimy piece of oyster right in front of Gaby's mouth.

"No, thank you."

"How come you never try my food, but I always try yours?" I asked.

"It's not part of my culture," Gaby replied.

"What about desserts? You always try my desserts."

"That's different. I like desserts," Gaby answered.

I didn't reply since I was still checking my heartbeat. "Shit, it is now a hundred thirty Can we go? I'd like to have sex before I die."

"The oysters are working already?" Gaby sounded skeptical.

"Don't mock me. It really works. It just takes a while."

I started to remove my wallet when Gaby stopped me. "I'm treating tonight."

"Thank you."

"That's the least I can do for a dying man," Gaby added.

It was a ten-minute, heart-monitoring taxi ride to our apartment. We waited for the elevator in the lobby of our Midtown East apartment. Paco, the congenial, overweight doorman, waited with us. "How was your dinner?" he asked.

"Excellent," Gaby answered.

"And yours, Dr. King?"

"I got a little indigestion," I replied.

"Sorry to hear that."

How come the doorman was more concerned about my health than my wife was?

The elevator finally arrived, and Paco held the door for us as he pressed the button for the fifth floor.

As the elevator door closed, I said, "I think the oysters are working."

"I can see that." Gaby was focused on my bulging crotch. I thrust my pelvis forward, proud of the tent that my erection created.

"I told you my period was over just yesterday," Gaby said. "It's not going to do any good—it's another week until I ovulate. Besides, I thought you were dying."

"I am," I answered. "But shouldn't you give a dying man his final request?"

Gaby grabbed my crotch and started kissing me passionately. We were still going at it as we stumbled through the hallway to our apartment. I fumbled with my keys to get in. Once inside the front door, we made our way toward the bedroom, removing our shoes and clothes along the way as we slid across the oak floor.

As we squirmed into the bedroom, I removed one pant leg, dragging the rest of my pants along the floor like a sloppy wedding-dress train. Gaby's dress was down to her waist. She pushed me onto the bed.

"Come to me, my little baguette," I said, speaking one of the few French words I had picked up in nearly two years of marriage. I grabbed Gaby's hand and pulled her toward me.

"Wait, I have to get the pillows ready," Gaby said.

"Really, now?" I complained.

Gaby had recently purchased what I called pregnancy-or-fuck pillows. They went under her back and raised her pelvis to the best angle to facilitate conception. What a turnoff, though, to stop in the middle of foreplay to fetch and set them up. I watched as she placed the pillows under her body until the angle was optimal, aligning them against her butt and the small of her back. It looked like she was doing Pilates. She stopped and gave me a nod. I prepared to mount.

"Wait," Gaby said as she sprang out of bed to open a window. Apparently fresh air and moonlight also helped conception.

What's with the feng shui? Let's just fuck, I thought.

Gaby got back in bed and into position all over again. "Okay, ready."

"Ready for what?" I asked. *"Cirque du Soleil?"*

"Don't make me laugh," Gaby said with a smile. "Just do me, cowboy."

Because I was from Colorado, Gaby thought I had to have cowboy blood in me. I think it was a French thing, a fascination with the Wild West. Wyatt Earp and Billy the Kid were legends to her. The fact that her husband, a Jewish dentist, came from that same untamed "Old West" country really amused her. When I first heard the cowboy reference, I nearly fell out of her vagina. Now I was used to it.

"Ride me, cowboy," Gaby coaxed. Then she looked at me funny. And that was the last thing I remembered.

CHAPTER 3

Too Much Mojo

OBVIOUSLY, I DIDN'T DIE FROM TOO MUCH SEX. I was in the hospital for two days. They ran every test imaginable. They even did an MRI. Everything was in perfect working order. The doctor called the episode vasovagal syncope. The ginseng, the liquids, the pills—I had simply overdosed on things they say you shouldn't overdose on. I was buzzing around like a hummingbird on speed. Mix in a lot of stress and the excitement from sex, it was no wonder I had passed out completely. My body needed a time-out.

"Just stop taking all that shit." That was the cure advised by Larry, an MD and one of my oldest friends. "It doesn't do anything."

I estimated that I had spent over $1,000 on "all that shit." Shit that didn't get us pregnant but did feel good to throw in the trash. After a few days, I felt normal again.

"Thank you," Gaby said as we both lay in bed reading.

"For what?" I asked.

"For trying so hard." She kissed me and then went back to her book.

Gaby felt like she had been the only one pushing to get pregnant, but once she found out what I had done, her concern turned to gratitude. Gratitude that I was on board. That I would go to such lengths to make it happen. Yet when she suggested acupuncture as a way to help us get pregnant, I was a little reluctant. Despite being a dentist, I was wary of any profession that had the word "puncture" in its job title.

I injected people with novocaine, not punctured them as if they were car tires. And where exactly was this acupuncturist going to aim? "So he's going to stab me in my dick?" I asked.

"You're being ridiculous," Gaby said. "They placed these very thin needles in my abdomen and around here." She pointed to her pelvic area. "I don't think it will be anywhere near the dicky—I mean, unless it's moved."

"Very funny," I said. "You don't think, but you're not sure."

"All right, I heard they stick you in the balls," Gaby added.

"What?" I said.

"I'm just kidding," Gaby said. "It's nothing."

I sat in the exam room as I waited for the acupuncturist, Dr. Chan. I wondered if he would look like the fiend from *Hellraiser,* with multiple metal piercings coming out of his big, bald head.

Dr. Chan didn't look anything like that. Soft-spoken, with a heavy Chinese accent, he gave me a reassuring smile as he took my wrist and placed two fingers on it. He paused as if he was listening for something.

"Do you have trouble urinating?" he asked.

"No," I said, not expecting that question.

He listened for a few more seconds. "Kidneys weak, drink more water," he said, and removed his hand from my wrist.

"Okay," I responded.

That's it? Drink more water? That was the solution to getting pregnant? How much was I paying for that bit of advice? At barely a sentence, that was like twenty-five dollars a word.

"Take off your shoes and socks and get on table," Dr. Chan said.

All right, here it comes.

I began to unzip my pants. I knew what was next.

"What you doing?" he asked.

"Well, getting ready for, you know . . . for you to puncture me," I said. "My abdomen and pelvis? Nothing else, right?"

He smiled, but for his reserved disposition it was probably akin to a belly laugh.

"No, not there," Dr. Chan said. "We have many doors to increase your chi."

I felt like an idiot as I quickly zipped up my pants. I bet his colleagues were going to get a laugh out of this at the next acupuncture convention. *Hey, you think that's funny? I know this dentist who thought I would stick him in the cock. What a schmuck!*

I felt even more foolish as Dr. Chan started lightly pricking the skin around my feet, hands, and head with super-thin needles. I could barely feel it. He turned down the lights.

"Back in twenty minutes," he said as he gently closed the door on the now-candlelit room. I just lay there in the quiet. *Now what? This was what thousands of years of Eastern medicine was all about? Where's the pain? Isn't it "no pain, no gain"?*

The worst part was having to lie there alone, waiting and hoping that whatever was happening would help. It was meditative: my mind would wander from my dick to work, to Gaby, to friends, to trivia, and then back again to my dick. How would all those little needles coming out of my hands, feet, and head signal my twin testicles to increase production? "Come on, guys," I imagined a coach saying to rally his players. "Fertilize!" I tried to relax, thinking that would somehow help the magical process. *Fertilize, fertilize, fertilize!*

I had five sessions with Dr. Chan (with lots of sex at home with Gaby in between), and each session seemed to involve more punctures. After several menstrual cycles had come and gone, we gave up on the acupuncturist.

"If you stop thinking about getting pregnant, it will fucking happen." Another bit of advice from Richard. "After our last kid, we thought we were done. Then when you least expect it, another fucking mouth to feed."

Apparently, a relaxed body is more likely to reproduce than a tense one. It made sense. So the trick was to forget we were trying to conceive. But when I tried not to think about it, I thought about it even more. I needed to dissociate from the word "baby." I tried a game. Whenever "baby" came into my head, I'd think about basketball. The mom on the street was pushing a stroller with a basketball inside. When we had sex, it was to make a basketball.

"Basketball. Basketball," I repeated.

"What are you whispering?" Gaby asked as we prepared to have sex in the middle of the afternoon.

"Nothing," I lied.

"I thought I heard you say 'basketball.'"

"No, I didn't."

"Yes, you did!"

"I'm trying not to think about why we're having sex," I said.

"So, we're having sex for a basketball?"

"No, for a baby. 'Basketball' is just so I can clear my mind of 'baby.' That way I'll be more relaxed. Less pressure."

"That's nuts." Gaby shook her head as we lay down in the bed.

We started kissing and she stopped. "I'm thinking 'basketball' now, too."

"Let's just fuck," I said.

"Good idea."

"You know when you stop thinking about getting pregnant?" I said to Richard a few days later.

"Tell me," Richard said.

"When you already have three kids!" I said. "That was the worst advice."

"Try visualization then," Richard suggested.

"So let me get this straight," I said. "Instead of *not* thinking about babies, now that's *all* you want me to think about?"

"Yeah. I read about visualization a long time ago and tried it with this babe I wanted to bang from my college contemporary-history class. That's all I thought about. Talking to her in class. Driving to her home. Laughing with her after sex. Meeting her parents. I mean later, not right after sex. And then one day she sat right next to me."

"And you had sex?" I asked.

"No! But the point is, it worked. She came to me. She sat next to me. I attracted her to come to me, in my mind. Women, babies, it's all the same thing. Just visualize."

I visualized shooting a bullet through Richard's head for all his bullshit advice. It didn't work. He was still alive.

Visualization was something I knew about. It was worth a try. And so I visualized coming home from work and seeing the baby in his or her nursery. I'd kiss the baby. I'd watch Gaby breastfeed with her huge lactating breasts (hey, my visualization, my rules). For weeks, I'd visualize every day of my life as if the baby were there. But nothing changed. Thinking about it, not thinking about it—all crap. They were mere acts of desperation in our trying-to-get-pregnant book.

Gaby was also getting tired of the lack of results. She didn't have to verbalize it. I could see it on her face: a look of exasperation, an aura of futility. But doing nothing was not an option. It meant defeat. Gaby was a fighter. That was how she got ahead in life. She did her home-work, worked harder than anyone else, and moved ahead. Why should pregnancy be any different for her? One way or another, she would find the way.

Gaby's coworker Ellen had had trouble conceiving for years until she started seeing a psychiatrist who specialized in "pregnancy issues." Ellen swore by him, because after only a few sessions with Dr. Ernest Lamardi, she became pregnant.

"Ellen said he's a miracle doctor!" Gaby exclaimed to me. "He's helped so many women. You see, deep down, we're fearful of being moms, of the responsibility."

Now, that sounded familiar to me.

"And that fear can keep us from getting pregnant," Gaby continued. "So he unblocks it all."

"Sounds great," I agreed, but I didn't believe it. A miracle doctor? I'd never heard of a pregnancy shrink. It had to be a scam.

Unblocks? Yeah, by hypnotizing vulnerable women and having sex with them. I read the tabloids. If Gaby gets pregnant while seeing him, I want a DNA test.

It seemed to me that people who had trouble getting pregnant treated it like a terminal illness. They would try anything to find a cure. For Ellen, the psychiatrist was the cure, and Gaby was convinced it would work for her also. She made an appointment.

Dr. Ernie talked to Gaby every Monday and Thursday from 2:00 to 2:50 p.m. What, a full-hour appointment was too long? They needed a break after just fifty minutes? They talked about Gaby's family; my family; her past, present, and future; all woven together with the thread of motherhood and how it related to her life. She resolved issues, made conclusions about her life, but the most important conclusion she walked away with was that she was ready for a child. I didn't realize she had also been in doubt like me: fearful of having a child, of the responsibility. Maybe everyone was, even if only a little. Gaby needed someone, an objective third party who was not a friend or family member, to tell her what we already knew—that she'd be a great mom. That whatever issues she had, with her distant father or her real mom who died way too young, didn't matter. She had to rise above all that fear to embrace the joy that came with self-confidence about motherhood. That alone was worth the price of admission. Dr. Ernie was legit.

Still, why would I need to talk to him? What was he going to tell me that I didn't already know? *I'm scared and selfish . . . okay, nice talking to you.*

"I don't want to see your shrink," I protested to Gaby after she asked.

"But he said it's important for him to talk with both of us," she countered.

I'd seen shrinks before. I had issues: and who wouldn't if their dad owned the most famous strip club in Denver, Colorado, and was called the Sultan of Striptease? And what if your mom, who was raised as an Orthodox Jew, managed his strip club? Would that psychologically mess you up or what? It was a miracle I wasn't living on some funny farm.

My psychiatrist never gave me straight answers to my issues. What she did give me was the insight to figure things out on my own. Psychiatrists are sneaky that way.

For Gaby's sake, I went to see Dr. Ernie for two sessions. It wasn't that much different from those sessions I had gone to years before. Only this time I was happily married and head-over-heels in love with my wife. I felt I had come a long way in dealing with commitment issues, but I had a ways to go. Peter Pan was still in the building.

Now my indecisiveness was about a different kind of relationship, one that involved a child. I didn't mention that to Dr. Ernie, but maybe he sensed my fear and reluctance about the whole thing. The message he did get from me loud and clear was this: "I'm crazy in love with Gaby and will do whatever I can to make her happy."

Dr. Ernie responded with a psychiatric nod of approval.

Would my love for Gaby allow me to overcome my fear of having a child? I hoped so.

PART II

CRAZY IN LOVE

CHAPTER 4

The One

Five years before all this, I was afraid I'd never get married. And then it happened, just like friends said it would—when I least expected it.

Did I know Gaby was the one? Was it like in the storybooks?

"I was eating a chile relleno at La Bonita's, and I looked up and there she was—the woman I was going to marry," Richard told me after he first saw his strikingly blond wife-to-be, Sandra. "Just like that," he said, snapping his fingers. "I knew she was the one—my fucking soulmate." He said that about every woman he was attracted to. If he said it often enough, it was bound to really happen one day— he'd meet the woman who would become The One.

I'd even said it once or twice when I was younger. Was there even just one right woman for every man? Maybe there were many people out there who could be The One. And how long were you supposed to wait? What if by the time I met her I was so old that I died the next day? Now, that would suck.

By the time I finally met my future wife, there was no bolt of light-ning that jolted my heart and made me think I'd finally met my one and only. Sure, there was that nervous shortness of breath, the butter-flies in the stomach that everyone gets when they meet a potential love interest. But I'd been there before.

Still, meeting Gaby was miraculous. It was one of those events in life so significant that I remember them as if they happened yesterday: my first kiss, the first time I drove a car, and the first glimpse I had of the woman I would one day marry.

I was at La Belle Époque, a French restaurant in Greenwich Village. It was tango night. I didn't tango, and neither did my two friends, Tara and Charles. We just thought it might be fun to watch, maybe even try it.

I noticed Gaby as the hostess escorted her party to their table. She was stunning. She took my breath away. I stared as long as I could as she walked past our table—long enough to notice that she wasn't wearing a wedding ring.

Maybe she's available, I thought.

They were seated right behind us—no more than five feet away.

What luck. She's so close. I have to give it a try.

In those situations, you maybe got one shot to attempt to meet the woman. I didn't want to blow it.

The tango music started as if signaling me that it was time to make my move. Even though I wasn't shy when it came to meeting women, I was still nervous. There was that ever-present possibility of rejection—no matter how confident I was. Boyfriends, mismatched sexual orientation, an outright *fuck off,* these were all possible outcomes. But the feeling of not trying was worse. What was the expression, "you snooze, you lose"? I had snoozed many times and regretted it. Richard had said to me countless times, "There goes another woman I'll never fuck." It was his way of saying *she got away.*

As the tempo to the tango music increased, I stood as if on cue in part of a movie scene. *Action!* I turned around, trying not to be conspicuous, at first looking up at the ceiling and then slowly down at the women sitting at the nearby table. Gaby was looking over her menu. Perfect. Now was the time, before the food came, before she got involved in some conversation with her friend. Now! I took two short steps to her table and butted into their space.

"Try the cod," I said. "It's very good."

Cod? That was the best you could come up with? You idiot.

I went with simple. Simple seemed the best.

She glanced up from her menu. It wasn't exactly a welcoming glance. I'm not unattractive: perhaps cute, of small stature, and in a lineup of pick-the-Jew, I'd be chosen near the top. I have that non-threatening look. Maybe it's due to the small, oval, look-like-a-doctor glasses that I wore. Well, actually they were my look-like-a-dentist glasses, ones that somehow I thought made me look more intellectual and less threatening. You wouldn't want a dentist with a menacing look coming at you with a needle dripping with lidocaine.

She turned toward me. It wasn't a good look. It was definitely a what-the-fuck-do-you-want look.

"Well, I hate the cod," she said in a such a way that she didn't have to add, "Now, leave me alone, buddy."

I would have left it at that, but I was instantly smitten by her thick French accent. Even a word like "hate" sounded so much better in French. Like Gomez Addams from the 1960s *Addams Family* television show, who melted every time Morticia spoke French, I had a weakness for the accent. I had to say something, but I was at loss for words.

"Nice talking to you, too," I said, and turned back to my friends.

"Way to go, stud," Charles said, augmenting my ridicule. His wife, Tara, chuckled, adding further to my humiliation.

She really had shut me down.

I shouldn't have gone with the cod. How many people hate cod?

I tried to filter out the noise from the rest of the tables around us so I could hear her table's conversation, maybe get a clue as to my next move. If I had one. Although they spoke French, I could make out a few words here and there. I was certain I heard "American" and "asshole" sprinkled in amid all the French. I wasn't sure which person said it.

We finished our meal and were ordering dessert. Although it seemed hopeless, I had to give it another try. I already felt like shit: feeling a little shittier wouldn't be a big deal. We wouldn't be there much longer. It had to be now or never.

Buying them drinks seemed too cliché. I had to try for bigger, something special. "What is your best, most delicious desert?" I asked the waitress.

"I like the chocolate-covered strawberries with zabaglione cream," she answered.

Who doesn't?

"Could you please send one of those over to the table behind me with the two women?" I asked, nodding in a backward direction with my head. "One of them has reddish hair, and they are speaking French."

The waitress glanced at the table behind us. "Of course," she said.

We got our desserts. I ate mine, slowly. I might have been eating air, I was so distracted. I was waiting for her to respond. I figured at some point, she'd thank me for the dessert. That zabaglione was a winner. What kind of person wouldn't thank you for sending them over strawberries and cream? Apparently, not the stunning French woman. Maybe it was a French thing. They didn't dish out thanks the lavish way we did here. It was cultural, not personal. That was what I hoped.

We paid the check. I stalled as long as I could.

"It's now or never," Charles said. "We'll wait for you over there by the bar."

He was right, it was now or never. I stood, turned, and then took a step toward the two women's table. I abruptly stopped. They were eating chocolate cake. *What the fuck!* I just stood there like an idiot. She must have sensed me staring at her, because she glanced over to where I was standing. I must have looked upset.

"I hate strawberries," she said. "So we got the chocolate cake instead."

Cod and now the strawberries. She hated everything!

"Oh," I said dumbly as I was about to turn and walk away forever.

"But thank you anyway," she added. "That was quite nice of you."

Not just nice—she had said *quite* nice.

Yes!

I screamed it in my mind but it came out, "You're welcome. I'm Michael, by the way." I extended my arm for a handshake.

There was clearly hesitation on her part. It felt like days were passing.

Take my damn hand already, I thought. *Please, don't humiliate me any more.* I waited. *Pretty please.*

And then, at last, she took my hand.

"Gabriella," she added as we touched for the very first time.

"And this is Nathalie," she added.

I don't care. I only have eyes for you. Come to me, my Gabriella.

I shook Nathalie's hand. But it was one of those obligatory handshakes accompanied by a half smile. I needed to give all my attention to Gabriella. I loved that name, Gabriella—so exotic.

Meeting a potential date was a lot like sales. You had just so long to seal the deal. My friends were impatiently waiting, so it had to be fast. I'd heard of speed-dating, where people went from one person to another and had a timed exchange to see if they wanted to make a date or not. They had just a few minutes to make their best pitch. Strong eye contact and then, "I graduated Yale, then Harvard Law, clerked for a Supreme Court chief justice, took a year off to help build a school in Ethiopia, and now I'm about to make partner with the firm My Shit Don't Smell." My pitch wasn't nearly that good: *USC undergraduate, Temple Dental School, pay fifteen dollars a month to sponsor one child with Save the Children, and now I'm talking to you.* Wasn't honesty the best policy? Bullshit walks or something like that? I had to go with honest.

"You're so gorgeous," I began. "Would you consider getting together for milk and cookies with a dentist-slash-stand-up-comedian?"

Who was on An Evening at the Improv *and other TV shows, opened countless times for Ray Romano and other famous comedians, sold a screenplay, and that's just the beginning,* I added, but only in my mind. The thing with sales, you've got to know when not to reveal too much. You can't be too eager, too desperate for the sale. More is less. The best salespeople reveal just enough so you want more.

Gabriella then turned to her friend, and I heard "Michael" at least twice and "dentist" once. I waited. From the tone of Nathalie's voice, she objected to the milk-and-cookie date. Why?

It had to be my age. Of late, my age had been a factor; I'd been hearing "You're too old for me" a lot. I was in my early fifties. Gabriella looked no older than thirty-one. It had to be an age thing. I had this theory that you could date people who were younger as long as your net worth was $50,000 per year of age difference. In other words, for a twenty-year age gap, you would need to be worth at least $1 million. Going by that theory, I didn't have a chance. I needed some luck.

Please don't listen to your friend, I thought, and gave off my best "choose me" smile.

Gabriella turned back to me. It was decision time.

"Tell me a joke," she said.

Was this an audition? Comedians hate it when someone asks them to tell a joke. We tell jokes onstage—that is our office. Or what is even worse is when someone volunteers to tell you a joke that they think you should use for your act. And they are usually the worst jokes in the world. Everyone thinks they're a comedian. Go to a comedy club, wait in line for three fucking hours for a number, and then deliver your lame-ass joke onstage yourself. Gaby had just committed a cardinal sin in the comedy world. But she was French; maybe they didn't know about those things.

Look at her. Just tell her a damn joke. She's worth it.

"I was walking into Bloomingdale's the other day," I opened, "and this annoying woman was right behind me. 'Coming through!'

she yelled. 'Coming through!' So I held the door for her. It was a revolving door."

I waited for the laugh—nothing from either of them. That was one of my best jokes, but not a chuckle. I'd even have settled for a smile. Nothing but a look of bewilderment.

What the fuck. I'm bombing here. Lost in translation?

"I don't get it," Gabriella said. She then turned to her friend, and they were obviously discussing the joke in French.

I felt like I was watching the Olympics when the international judges were talking over a point dispute. My simple, well-constructed, time-tested joke was being judged by two thickly accented French women I'd just met. This was a comic's nightmare.

Gabriella turned toward me. "I get it now," she said. "It is funny," she added with a slight grin.

"Thanks," I said, thinking some people must laugh on the inside.

"Do you have a pen?" she asked.

I heard the angels sing hallelujah in my mind.

It worked. It was a great joke. This is so much better than getting twenty dollars for a weekday spot at the Broadway Comedy Club.

As a bona fide nerd, I always carried a pen in my pocket, which I whipped out. Gabriella tore off a small piece of the paper table covering and wrote her number. I looked at it. Ten digits. Ten digits that might as well have been a secret code to a safety deposit box in Geneva that held $1 million.

This little piece of paper is mine. All mine! Gabriella, please come home with me, now. Let's not play any more games.

"Thank you," I said. "Very nice to meet you both." I walked quickly away, not wanting to deliver another joke or hear my name mixed in with French.

"Well?" Charles asked.

I proudly displayed the piece of paper with the number on it.

CHAPTER 5

Fooked Up

"Do you think she gave you her real number?" Richard later asked me over the phone.

"Shit," I answered. "I didn't think of that."

"Sometimes they'll give you a fake number, just to get rid of you. Like for the post office or the zoo."

I was sure Richard was speaking from experience.

I'd never gotten a fake number before. Maybe I was just lucky.

Has my luck run out?

I would wait a week to find out. "Women hate neediness," I once was told by Barbara, a good friend of mine. "There's no bigger turnoff than a guy who's being too eager. I hate it when some guy tells me his life story after I've known him for one minute, or calls me back too soon."

What's too soon? A day? Some say wait a week. Isn't that too long?

It was a battle with myself. I put the number away. And that was all I thought about all week, calling Gabriella.

Six p.m. on a Thursday, I sat in front of my phone.

Thursday was close enough. Tomorrow it would be a week. I can't call her on Friday night. Who calls to make a date on a Friday? Someone like her would never be home then.

I tapped in the number and it rang. At least it was some real number.

It still could be the zoo.

It rang again and again and . . .

"Oui?" said the voice on the other end of the line. Hearing a female, definitely French voice was very encouraging.

"Gabriella?" I asked, still not certain.

"Oui, I mean, yes," she answered, switching to English.

OMG, it's really her! I couldn't believe it. I was so excited, I could have done a backflip if I'd known how.

"This is Michael; I met you at the restaurant last week. I bought you the dessert . . . well, not exactly. I bought you strawberries, but you hate strawberries."

"I don't know who you are," Gabriella said.

Are you shitting me?

"Really?" I said. "I was with two—"

"What, the comedian who can't take a joke?" she interrupted me. "Of course I remember you."

I laughed. "You got me."

And that was how it all started. The first date: a French bistro and a kiss on the cheek. (Here's a tip: a cheek kiss on the first date shows confidence and lack of neediness.) The second date: Italian food, a movie, and a kiss on the lips. The third date: a Broadway play, then pizza, after which she invited me up to her place and we had some make-out action. As I left, she said, "I have to get up early."

The fourth date: my place. I pretended to cook but really ordered out Greek. I did light some candles, set the table, and uncork the wine. We drank, we talked until after two a.m., and then we kissed and kissed and made love. I do mean love. I was already in love with her.

"I like you, Gaby," I said as we lay in bed.

"Who told you that you could call me Gaby?" she said, very annoyed. "Only my parents and brother are allowed to call me that."

"Sorry, Gabriella, my mistake."

"It's okay. I like Gaby from you. And I like you, too."

I smiled a dumb-ass smile, as if we had reached some milestone in our relationship.

"But I don't get it," she added.

I quickly stopped smiling, fearful of what was to follow the word "but."

"Get what?"

"You're, what? Forty-one or forty-two, I guess?"

Here it goes.

"Close enough," I said, not quite ready to reveal my true age.

"You're nice, you're funny, even though I don't get all the jokes. You're a dentist. Why aren't you married? Are you *fooked* up?"

"No, I'm not *fooked* up."

"Then what?"

"Do you want the simple or complex answer?"

"Simple first, to see if I believe you," she said.

I took a deep breath. "I never found the right one," I said.

Until I met you.

"Dog shit," she said.

"The term is 'bullshit,'" I said. Even though Gabriella had worked for an international organization in its information services for over ten years and was fluently multilingual, she still hadn't mastered some of the nuances of colloquial English.

"Bullshit, dog shit, whatever shit," she said, "tell me the truth."

"It's complex," I added.

"I've got time. I'm not going anywhere. Unless you want me to go?"

"No, no, don't go. I never want you to go. I mean, not tonight. You can leave in the morning, when we both go."

I took a deep breath and tried to explain. "I told you about my dad and the strip joint," I began.

"Yes, the dancing ladies came to the synagogue and sat watching you *ba-mitz* in their sexy dresses, and the Jewish men were all distracted. Do you talk about that in your act?"

"I should. Anyway," I continued, "I read this article a shrink wrote about men who never married. Don't get me wrong. I do want to get married someday. I definitely do. But the article talked about fathers who weren't around a lot. Like my dad. What happens is that the mothers have to play the dual roles—the father and the mother. So the mom has to be loving and nurturing but also macho and strong. She has to be all things. That's a hard act to follow. So for men who have been raised like this, no woman—unless it's their mother—is good enough for them. Maybe that's why they say that men marry their mothers. I mean, you're not anything like my mother. Not that that would be important at this stage."

"I don't buy it," Gaby said. "I don't need some psychiatrist to explain it. *C'est simple.* Most men are immature and afraid to give up their freedom. They think only about what they'll lose, not what they'll gain. You're a baby and afraid to commit."

"That sounds good also," I said. "I can buy that."

Much simpler, too.

"By the way, how old are you, really?" Gaby asked.

"Seventy-seven—I have good genes," I said.

From the look on her face, she didn't suffer fools or bad jokes.

All right. I have to tell her sometime. If she bolts, she bolts. Better now than later. Honesty is the best policy.

"I am fifty-two—well, almost fifty-three," I said.

So long, nice knowing you.

"Okay, not so bad," Gaby said.

Are you shitting me? That was it? God bless the French. Relationships are ageless.

CHAPTER 6

Commitment

GABY AND I HAD BEEN DATING FOR TWO MONTHS. We flew out to my cousin's wedding in Southern California. We had some free time during the day and decided to take a hike in a canyon just northwest of San Diego.

There was a large sign on the trailhead in big, bold letters that read BEWARE OF RABIES along with other warnings: loose gravel, ticks, mountain lions, and more. We both spent a minute reading the sign. After about ten minutes or so of hiking on the trail, Gaby stopped at a clearing and looked around. She seemed confused.

"Honey, where are the rabbis?" she asked.

I started laughing.

"What?" Gaby asked. "What's so funny?"

"Rabies," I answered, trying to contain my laughter. "The sign said beware of *rabies,* not rabbis."

"*Oui,*" Gaby said. "That makes more sense."

Then she started laughing too and got me laughing even more. We couldn't stop. Our shared laughter became so intense, it not only hurt my ribs and brought tears to my eyes, but somehow bound me closer to her. That moment for me was the icing on the cake. That was the moment I knew for certain what I had to say.

"Gaby, I love you," I said for the first time out loud.

"Are you talking to me?" Gaby asked.

"Very funny," I said.

"Can you take it back?" she asked.

I was not happy with her reply. "Really, why?"

"Because I wanted to say it first," she added, much to my relief.

I quickly complied. "I take it back. It never happened," I said. "All right, I'm waiting."

"Michael, I love you," Gaby said with a look that left no doubt in my mind that she meant it.

"And I love you, too," I said.

We kissed and kissed. It didn't matter if there were mountain lions, ticks, or rabbis nearby. We were in love and that was all that mattered.

I have this theory. I have a lot of them. After nearly forty years of dating and observing relationships, you can't help but come up with some theories. Sure, there are always exceptions to any generalization. But I was fairly certain that to take a relationship to the next level of commitment, whether it be cohabitation, engagement, marriage, or just saying, "I love you," there had to be one special thing that made that other person remarkable in your eyes.

That special thing could be something simple: the way they laughed, how generous they were, or their unbelievable tattoos. Lots of money, big breasts, or a large penis are special enough for some.

For me, smart, French, and beautiful were all great. Gaby was fluent in French, English, and Spanish, traveled the world for her job, and owned her own apartment. She was from the A-list.

I also loved the way Gaby confused things. She called goose bumps "pimples from the goose" and said "paralyzed parking" when she saw a handicapped parking slot. That one was my favorite.

All that was endearing. But there was something more, something deeper that made her so special to me. She was a clear-eyed, confident woman with a razor-sharp focus, determined to have a quality life with a minimum of hassle and bull. She didn't question and analyze everything like I did. She was a no-nonsense babe who called it like she saw it. If she'd had a tattoo on her thigh, it would have said, "Don't bullshit me." She knew what she wanted and needed in her life. That was the special thing that removed any doubt about my feelings for her.

I still can't say for sure what Gaby saw in me: a short, older Jew who had trouble making decisions. I did have a successful business, and I made her laugh. I once read that humor is the number-one thing that women are attracted to in a mate. (I think a broke comic said that.) Whatever it was, I thanked God for her. I felt astonishingly lucky and blessed that I had found her.

Before I met Gaby, I had dated several women who married the next guy they met after we broke up. That could be taken several ways. Either I made them so miserable that the next guy seemed great, or I showed them what "special" was, and with the next guy they knew exactly what they wanted. At one point I wanted to put it on social media: "Go out with me and I can guarantee you'll marry the next guy." With Gaby I didn't want to make that mistake, I didn't want to lose her, even if there was no indication of that happening. I didn't want to take a chance. I wanted her to know that she was the one I wanted to spend my life with.

After three months of dating, of sleeping some nights at her place and other nights at mine, she moved in with me. It seemed so natural. We both were tired of bringing stuff back and forth to each other's apartment. We were tired of spending Sunday nights apart because work was on Monday; of returning from a vacation and having to go back to our respective apartments. I hated all of it. We just wanted to be together, every day. That made us both happy.

And we were outstandingly happy together. At night in bed, I'd sometimes stare at her while she slept. I knew it seemed a little creepy, but I just couldn't believe she was there, with me. Sometimes she sensed I was looking at her and she opened her eyes slowly.

"What?" she would ask in a weak, groggy voice.

"I can't believe how beautiful you are," I would answer.

Gaby would smile and close her eyes. "Go to sleep, honey."

We had been together almost a year, and the word "marriage" was coming up a lot—not so much with us, but with friends and family. "When are you guys getting married?" friends would ask. "When are you going to make an honest man out of him?" my uncle Harry said to us on a trip to Denver. That was something an eighty-eight-year-old uncle would say.

"Very soon," Gaby answered.

"Really?" I asked. "You're ready to get engaged?"

"Yes, you idiot," Gaby said. "And you're not?"

Warning, it's a trick question. Answer it how she would answer it.

"Of course I am," I answered. "Let's do it." Gaby and I kissed.

"And you're both very welcome," Uncle Harry said, praising himself for the intervention that finally got us to make a commitment.

It was that simple. Without a formal ceremony or fireworks, but with just a simple kiss, we were engaged. *That's it? I don't feel any different.*

But it wouldn't be official until I got a ring. All the men I talked to about getting engaged mentioned the spending rule. The amount you should spend on the engagement ring should be two or three months' salary. What genius jeweler concocted that one?

"Yeah, that's correct," Richard confirmed. "But it's retail value, not wholesale. Luckily, I was only making about $400 a week at the time. So I only had to pay around $4,000 for her ring. But with your income, you're fucked."

"Thanks," I said.

"And another tip," Richard continued. "Don't surprise her: they know what ring they want. Let her pick it out."

Yours and Mine Jewelers was on Thirtieth Street in Manhattan. I had asked a bejeweled patient where a good place was to get an engagement ring. She knew this guy, Nick, who had beautiful discounted stuff. Discounted sounded good, especially considering the spending rule.

"What are you looking for?" Nick asked.

"A ring," I answered. That was all I knew for sure. I was in the dark about anything else.

Gaby, unbeknownst to me, had done her research. She whipped out a piece of paper with a sketch on it.

Holy shit! She caught me completely off guard.

"I've been searching online and I prefer something like this," she said to Nick as he looked at the picture. "Something simple, but art deco."

"I like it," Nick said. "And what kind of stone are you thinking of?"

"I like the natural yellow diamond for the main stone, and alternating yellow and white for the baguettes," Gaby added.

I had no idea what they were talking about. *Can you speak fucking English, please?*

"What cut?" Nick asked, happy he was talking to someone who spoke jewelerese.

"What do you think of the princess cut?" Gaby asked.

"Great choice. And size?" Nick asked.

"Nothing too big: two carats or less," Gaby answered. "Is that okay with you, honey?"

"Sure," I answered. "Sounds good to me."

"No problem," Nick said as I watched him open the door and walk into the nearby vault.

There are a lot of diamonds out here, in these glass cases. Why is he walking into the vault? And what does "princess cut" mean? One monster diamond costing a king's ransom? Am I fucked?

"He has such lovely jewelry," Gaby said, looking into the case.

Yeah, but apparently not good enough for a princess.

Nick returned with a plush-felt jeweler's display tray with several yellow diamonds scattered on top.

"They're so beautiful," Gaby said. "Aren't they, honey?"

"Yes, they are," I said.

Three months' salary? These look more like three years' salary. Is that after or before sales tax?

"I really like this one," Gaby said.

"It's very nice, isn't it?" Nick pulled out his jeweler's loupe for a closer look. "That's a GIA-rated fancy yellow, just under two carats."

"What do you think?" Gaby asked.

It's bigger than your knuckle. Can you get something smaller?

"If that what's you want," I answered. "Let's get it."

"Wonderful," Nick said. "It will take about—"

"I don't want to know when it will be ready," Gaby declared. "That part I want to be a surprise."

CHAPTER 7

Rock My World

It was July, a crazy hot time to be in Arizona. It was nearly two months after Gaby had picked out her ring. If she was concerned as to when I'd give it to her, she hid it well. Still, Gaby had to be nervous. Like children playing "Pop Goes the Weasel," Gaby knew a surprise was coming; she just didn't know when I'd pop big the question and produce the ring.

I had it all planned. A trip to Arizona to visit my aunt and uncle. Since I was close to them, it didn't seem out of the ordinary that we'd pay them a visit even if it was July.

"Sure, we'll keep the ring," Aunt Sue said when I told her I was shipping it to her. I thought it was safer, with less chance of Gaby discovering it, if I had the jewelry store send the ring out to Arizona rather than carried it myself.

And I don't have to pay New York sales tax if I ship it out of state. You cheap bastard.

We spent two nights in Phoenix. Uncle Jack kept Gaby busy while Aunt Sue took me to a secret spot in her closet. Under several shoes was a hidden floor safe. Sue opened it and handed me a wrapped box.

"Show me, please, show me," she said in an excited whisper.

I unwrapped and opened the box. Inside was a small ring case covered with black velvet. I opened it.

The center yellow diamond, surrounded by a dozen smaller diamonds, sparkled like a marquee that flashed, "Marry Me!"

Holy shit. It's really happening.

"Oh, my God!" Sue exclaimed a little too loudly. "It's gorgeous," she added in a whisper.

I've never heard men get as excited about engagement rings as women do. I've seen several women encircle an engagement ring, like vultures surrounding their prey, while their friend held out her hand for all to see. It reminded me of guys looking at porn. "Oh, my God, look at the size of that. It's so big. Can I touch it?"

Sedona, Arizona, was an easy drive from Phoenix. It is a special, laid-back, funky place, with more alleged spiritual vortexes than almost anywhere else in the world. Our hotel, the Enchantment Resort, was surrounded by mesas and bluffs straight out of an old western, and it even had one or more of those spiraling concentrations of spiritual energy itself. Vortexes supposedly can facilitate healing, praying, and oneness with the universe. Not a bad place to get engaged.

We walked on the red sandstone rocky bluff, a five-minute hike from the hotel.

"That's the closest vortex," the hotel concierge had said as he looked out the hotel lobby window and pointed to the spot where Gaby and I were now standing. We could see the hotel in the valley below under a blue sky sprinkled with billowy white clouds that seemed to hold a secret. Gaby was dressed to hike. The sun fell on her—nature's spotlight showcasing her beauty.

As Gaby took in the panorama, I looked around and up, trying to feel the power of the vortex, the energy of the universe concentrated in that spot. I felt something. I'm not sure what it was. *It's like the surface of the sun out here. It's so fucking hot.* But I did have to pee; maybe it was that. Or maybe it was just the anticipation and excitement of what I was about to do.

I reached into my pocket and took out the fake rubber rock, the kind you buy to hide keys, with its secret compartment that held the ring. I secretly dropped the rock, and it landed quietly on the soft dirt between two small succulent plants. I smiled. Things were going perfectly so far.

"I'm feeling something," I said. "It's this place. I'm having a vision."

"What are you talking about?" Gaby said as she turned toward me.

"In my head, I feel something," I added.

"Maybe you're getting a headache," Gaby said.

"No. It's definitely a vision," I said, trying to act the part of a seer. "It has to be from the vortex. I see a magic rock and there is something inside," I continued, touching the temples on my head as if I were adjusting my mind to see things more clearly.

"It must be the heat," Gaby said, a little concerned.

"No, there—you see that one there?" I pointed to my rubber fake rock.

"What are you talking about? There are lots of rocks," Gaby said as she started kicking them around, including mine. There was dust from flying dirt everywhere, and I could no longer see my fake one. *What the hell!*

"Stop!" I said. "You're upsetting my vision."

"What's with this vision? Maybe you need to see a doctor."

"Where's the damn rock?" I asked in panic.

I watch and waited, as the dust slowly cleared, not knowing if the bogus rock and ring were still there.

I think it's insured.

"Thank God it's still there," I said with great relief as the rubber one came back into view. "Please, Gaby, pick it up."

"Pick what up?" she asked.

"Right there," I said and pointed. "Just pick up the damn rock!"

Gaby went to get it as if she were indulging a person who was losing his mind.

"Yes, that's it. Pick it up!" I commanded.

"This?" she asked, now holding the phony stone. "It's nothing." She got ready to toss it.

"No, don't! There's something inside," I said. "Open it."

"It's made of rubber," Gaby observed, and she started to look suspicious.

"There's a slot," I said. "Please, just open it."

Gaby pulled and opened the concealed compartment.

"What's this?" she asked as she looked inside.

I watched her closely. For a moment, she frowned as if she was trying to figure out what she was looking at. Away from the jewelry store, tucked in a bizarre container, the ring had to seem foreign, out of context. I was counting on that. She then looked up and stared at me. Her eyes teared up as she knew for certain what it was. I got on one knee.

"Gaby, here in this special place, with the universe as our witness, will you marry me?" I asked.

"Yes, yes, a thousand yeses!" Gaby replied, and took out the ring from its compartment.

She started to cry. I started to cry. Through my tears I watched her put on the ring.

"It's even more beautiful then I'd imagined it would be," Gaby said.

I've never felt such joy in my entire life. From the look on her face, I could safely say she was feeling the same. The vortex seemed to be doing its job. It filled us both with the joy that only real love could bring. Then one of her tears landed on my forehead, as if she had anointed me and created a magical bond that could never be broken—a bond sanctified by the spiritual force of the earth's mystical powers.

CHAPTER 8

Mothers and Strippers

RELATIONSHIPS WERE ALWAYS EASIER WHEN your family was on board. My family loved Gaby. Sometimes I think they loved her more than they loved me.

Although it's true that the longer I waited to get married the less picky my mom was about whom I'd marry.

When I started dating, the girl had to be Jewish. Even though my mom managed a strip club, many of her core values had remnants of Orthodoxy. She insisted I should date only Jewish women. "Jews must stick together," she would say.

But Jews get divorced like everyone else, I wanted to tell her. Still, my sister Andie and I would have to keep it a secret if we were dating goyim.

"Who was that girl your cousin Dennis saw you with on Saturday night at the Center Theatre?" my mom asked me as if she was looking for a fight.

Denver is such a frigging village.

"Just a friend," I answered.

"Just a friend? Do you always hold hands with 'just a friend'? A blond, not-Jewish 'just a friend'?"

Ma, leave me alone. The girl is smart, pretty, and willing to have sex with me.

I knew of people whose families wouldn't talk to them for years or who disowned them because they married someone of another faith.

Some people, like my mom, still held on to the belief that same-faith marriages were more successful.

By the time I got engaged to Gaby, I was so old, all my mom cared about was that my wife was a mammal. *If she walks on land, son—if she has a spinal cord—invite the creature over to the house. You got my blessing.*

My dad never cared about such things. He loved Gaby from the start, and he even told her she'd make a "great dancer." For him that was the highest compliment you could bestow on a woman. I know it sounds demeaning and sexist, but not from my dad. He was genuinely in love with all women, and not in a romantic way. He lit up when a woman walked into the room. He found them smart, caring, and mysterious. He respected women and treated them with a sense of awe. He would rather spend time talking to a woman than a man. Was he an angel? Maybe that's for another book.

"Look at her, Michael," my dad said, watching Gaby as she walked with my mother in Greenwich Village while Dad and I strolled behind. "She's something else."

"Yes, she is," I agreed.

And Gaby loved my dad. She loved his enthusiasm, especially his French-like joie de vivre. He was a man who followed his heart.

Gaby also loved visiting my family in Denver, and with less than a year before the wedding, we decided to visit them—our last time as an engaged couple. We were headed back to their house after an early dinner with friends when Gaby out of nowhere blurted out what sounded like an order.

"I want to go to your papa's club."

"Now?" I asked, somewhat baffled.

"Yes, now, tonight," Gaby replied.

"Are you sure you want to go there?" I asked, more for myself than Gaby. I felt a little uncomfortable about taking her—I hadn't heard any good things about the place in a long time.

"Absolutely, honey," she said. "Is that okay?"

"Sure, that's fine," I replied, not wanting to show any anxiety. "No problem."

I hadn't been to Dad's club in years. Business wasn't good; I knew that. It was just a matter of time before the place would have to close. The stripping business had changed. Corporations ran Vegas-style strip joints, circuses of pole dances, lap dances, and gourmet steaks. The world-famous Sid King's Crazy Horse Bar had become passé. My dad could barely pay his bills. He was holding on, even though we encouraged him to declare bankruptcy.

Despite that, the flickering neon sign was still there. The "s" of KING'S was out, and the lights were much dimmer than I remembered.

The place looked run-down. The once-bright red-velvet wallpaper had lost its sheen. The stage seemed so much smaller than it once had. It was the same stage featured in a scene from Clint Eastwood's movie *Every Which Way but Loose*. My dad had a cameo in the film, and the orangutan had sat between him and Clint at the revolving bar—the first in America. But the bar no longer revolved. Many other celebrities had rested their butts on the now-faded black chairs and barstools: John Wayne, "Chill" Wills, Edd "Kookie" Byrnes, Elvis Presley, King Hussein, and (I'd heard) Walt Disney, to name a few.

Maybe Dad doesn't even want us here. Not now.

I couldn't have been more wrong. My dad seemed to light up when he saw us walk toward him. He was just getting ready to start the show. "Gaby," he boomed. "I'm so happy you're here! Take a seat over here, near me," he added, pointing at one of the many empty tables. "You're gonna love it here!"

It was as if I weren't even there.

"I'm sure I will," Gaby said, smiling at my dad.

I watched him pick up the microphone. He must have known the end was near, that he was fighting a losing battle, that the fame and notoriety of his strip-club days were behind him. The place was nearly empty.

But he opened with great enthusiasm anyway. "We got a great

show for you tonight," he said. "And if I embarrass you, that's good. We have a special guest, my soon-to-be daughter-in-law Gaby! Look at her! Isn't she gorgeous?"

I applauded, as did one other guy at the formerly revolving bar whom I recognized as one of Sid's old regulars. Gaby tried to smile as her eyes opened wide from embarrassment.

"Our first dancer was a virgin when Moses was in the Sinai," Sid continued.

There were only a few chuckles in the small audience, a mix of confused tourists talking to themselves and a few other regulars who looked as old and worn-out as the furniture.

"Her bra is so big it was made at the Colorado Tent and Awning Company."

Laughter, yes, real laughter this time from the audience.

"The one and only Tessy, the Tennessee Tassel-Twirler," Sid finished, and more laughter rang out.

Gaby stared as if she were watching a moon landing. Tessy twirled the tassels that were attached to her nipples: first the right breast one way, then the left breast another way, and then both breasts at the same time in opposite directions. Very talented.

"Don't try this at home, Gabriella," my dad added.

I wasn't certain what she was feeling—repulsion, amazement, or skepticism. *What am I marrying into?* Was she thinking that? Was it all too much for her to handle?

My family had been too much for girls before. I was thirteen, a few months after my bar mitzvah, when I called Barbara to ask her out for my first date ever. I'd had a crush on her since the third grade. It took a lot of courage for me to call her. I was so nervous as I rotary-dialed. It seemed like it took forever for someone to answer.

"Hello."

"Barbara?" I said in my squeaky, about-to-die voice.

"Yes," she replied.

"Hello, Barbara," I continued, barely able to breathe. "It's Michael

King, Barbara: sorry, I already said that. Do you want to go with me to the Jewish Community Center Lake Dance on Sunday? Barbara?"

"I'll have to ask my mother," she replied.

I was ecstatic that she didn't say no. She went to ask her mother.

"Is your father Sid King?" Barbara asked, returning to the phone. "Who owns that Crazy Horse place?"

"Yes," I answered, not thinking it was a bad thing.

"Well, my mom says the apple doesn't fall far from the tree," Barbara said.

"What apple? What tree?" I asked.

There was no reply, then a sudden deadly dial tone.

The love of my young life didn't want anything to do with me because of what my father did. I was devastated.

Looking at Gaby, I wondered. Was it happening all over again with the *real* love of my life?

I watched my dad closely: his movements, his excitement, his love for his work. I realized it didn't matter to him if there were nine people or 200 in the audience. His energy, his larger-than-life persona, shone like a beacon through a room of gloom. The people who sat there were drawn to him, to his light, to his passion—a passion so great he still connected with the old regulars, the few strangers, and Gaby. It validated him and those around him. It was contagious; we all felt it. Gaby turned to me with a large grin on her face.

Yes, she still loves me!

I saw something in Dad that night that I had failed to see before. He had discovered the simple truth that life begins whenever you let it. No matter what age you are, or the circumstances, sometimes you just have to let go of all the stuff and enjoy life like a child. Owning a strip joint—even a worn-out one—being a dentist, or whatever you do in life, it doesn't matter as long as you live with passion. To find fulfillment, you have to find the love in who you are, even if what you love marks you as different from everyone else. I had discovered my dad's treasure, his gift. That was my legacy. It was there all along. I just never saw it before. I smiled. I was so proud of him.

Gaby grabbed my hand and squeezed it.

I knew she was proud to be part of my family.

CHAPTER 9

Happy Wife, Happy Life

MY DAD DIDN'T MAKE IT TO THE WEDDING.

It is sad when someone you love passes before a memorable event. You want those very special people in your life to be there, to share in your joy. Dad died only a few months before the wedding. Maybe the bankruptcy, the loss of the club, had something to do with it. They found a tumor in his brain and he went quickly. He still kept his humor, his love of life, until near the end. Lying in his hospital bed, he suddenly opened his eyes.

"Michael, I finally figured it out," he said. "Do you know what's more important than money? Lots of cash." He then laughed.

That was one of the last things he said to me. It wasn't profound or insightful or an epiphany, just a simple funny thing to say. I like to think it was his way of saying, "It's all right. Laugh a lot, enjoy life, and you'll be okay."

When you get married late in life, you usually have to pay for the wedding yourself, because your parents either may be dead or don't remember who you are. So you do things to discourage people from coming, like holding it out of town—say, Baghdad—or like we did, in Texas. I had a much larger and closer family than Gaby. She had only a handful of close friends and a few coworkers who came to the wedding. Her father and stepmother weren't going to attend. They were always too ill to travel. They'd been ill as long as I'd known them. And her brother seemed to be a selfish schmuck, not interested in anything else other than his Elvis cover band.

None of that mattered, because Gaby had found a new home filled with a large, caring family. Of course, we had our black-sheep eccentric uncles and weird cousins, but even they knew that family came first. We were all there for one another. We were all there for Gaby. She was one of us now.

Austin was central for the seventy-five or so guests who mostly came from Texas, California, and Colorado. And it was much less expensive for everyone than holding it in New York City.

We took our vows under the chuppah in the sun-filled garden at Green Pastures Inn in Austin. I swear I could hear my dad's raspy voice in my head: *You did okay, Michael. I'm so proud of you, son. I'm so proud.* And then I heard a train whistle off in the background, as if the universe was in on it.

Gaby did a wonderful job managing all the wedding details, from the classical guitarist who did the music, to the favors: baseball caps with our initials, G and M, embroidered on the front. We took lessons for our first dance, to *You're Nobody 'Til Somebody Loves You* by Dean Martin. And I took secret singing lessons and surprised Gaby with the song *I Love Paris.* She cried, I cried, everyone cried. It was an outstanding wedding.

But a wedding is just the start of the real test: marriage. And there are certain rules that you don't discover until after you get married. These rules are not written anywhere but seem instinctive to wives. You don't even know there is a rule until you learn about it the hard way.

"You really like this apartment?" Gaby asked one evening as we were getting ready for bed.

We had been married about six months, and I loved her more each day. Gaby had agreed to continue living in my apartment for a while. A creature of habit, I was content to keep on living there. Like forever.

"I love it," I answered.

She gave me the look. It was the look that said, "You're fucking kidding me."

"I hate this apartment," Gaby said. "I feel like I'm living in a jail."

And then she added an even worse zinger. "The reason we don't have any cockroaches is that we don't have room for them."

That was when I learned one of the first rules of my marriage. When my wife asks a question, don't answer as *I* would answer, answer as *she* would. "I love it" was the wrong answer. A simple "No, I don't like this apartment" would have been much better.

I knew Gaby wasn't thrilled with my apartment, but hate? Sure, it was less than 400 square feet, so small you could open the front door from anywhere in the place. But it was cozy. And it was a rent-stabilized Gramercy Park apartment for under $1,000 a month. People in New York would kill for that. But none of that mattered; my wife wasn't happy living there, and a happy wife trumps cheap rent.

"Don't fight it or try to figure her out; just agree," Richard advised. "It's not worth it. In the end, you'll do what she wants anyway. Move the fuck out!"

Sick as it sounded, Richard was my go-to guy for marriage advice. He had a way of getting to the heart of the matter.

A month later we moved out. I had a twenty-year run of being single and irresponsible in that apartment. Twenty years of freedom had gone by in a flash. Certain events are a wake-up call that make you realize just how fast time is passing, and that was one of them. The movers had come and I was getting ready to close up shop. Gaby could see that I was upset.

"You want a few minutes alone?" she asked without being sarcastic. I appreciated that.

"If that's okay?" I asked.

"Take your time. I'll be downstairs," Gaby said, and then left me alone in the apartment.

God, she knows me so well. It's scary.

I stood in the empty space, right where the old couch used to be. The place looked sad. All that was left was dust and memories. "We had a good time, didn't we?" I asked. I waited for the walls to answer, but they remained silent, indifferent, waiting for a new paint job.

I turned off the lights, closed the door, and slid the keys back under it. The world of being single was completely lost to me now.

Richard taught me another rule of marriage. "You think your wife is your best friend?" he asked me one day.

"Absolutely," I answered.

"Bullshit," he countered. "You can't have sex with your best friend. Try saying to her, 'Let's make love, buddy,' 'Can I do you from behind, pal?' or 'Wanna suck on my dick, mac?' Your wife can never be your best friend. Having said that, always tell her she's your best friend."

Richard was right. There are things you do with your wife that you would never do with your best friend—like going to Costco.

Gaby loved that place because it sold in bulk. When I was single, I never went there. I'd buy a bar of soap and it would last for three years—and that was the trial size. But Gaby took me to Costco soon after we were married. For nine dollars, she bought what seemed like 500 rolls of toilet paper. There was no room in our apartment, just us and the toilet paper. I wanted to invite neighbors over just to shit.

Hi! We live next door. Would you like to come over for a cup of coffee and maybe take a crap while you're there? Here's some toilet paper.

Costco, the Container Store, Bed Bath & Beyond, and Crate & Barrel: these were just a few of the places where we spent hours and hours, buying stuff to make our new apartment feel like home. We even had to buy a new bed.

"I'm not sleeping on something where you *fooked* other women," Gaby said.

I was on a roll. I had made major life-changing decisions without exploding. I had an incredible wife, a good business, and now a big apartment in midtown Manhattan with lots of space.

Space for what—a baby perhaps?

Part III

Fertility Hell

CHAPTER 10

Spanking the Monkey

EXCEPT NO BABY WAS FORTHCOMING.

Nothing was happening. Nothing was working. Gaby knew it, too.

After two years of trying to conceive, we were left frustrated and exhausted in both body and spirit. It weighed heavily on us both.

"I feel like people at work are looking at me like something's wrong with me," Gaby said with a sigh one evening when she got home from work. "Like I'm sick because I can't get pregnant."

"Honey, nothing's wrong with you. It's just timing," I said, taking her hand. "We have to be patient. You'll see, it will happen."

Gaby sat quiet for a long moment before she spoke. "Maybe I was lying to myself about wanting to be a mother. Maybe I only thought that, because society says I should want to. "

You don't mean that, honey. You want to be a mother more than anything.

I knew what she was doing. She was trying to find a rationale for failure, looking for something, anything, to make the pain of a childless life palatable.

In that moment, my mind raced. I couldn't let her go down that path. None of this was her fault. She was in pain, and I couldn't let it continue. Was it my fault? Had my reluctance and fear somehow affected our ability to get pregnant? I needed to take on this fight right alongside Gaby—for us. Up until now I felt like I had only been shadowboxing, making the moves, but unwilling to take the real punches.

I had to put myself in the ring. *Quit being a fucking baby. Go for it! Become a dad.*

"Well, what about me?" I said. "I care what society says about me. And they're saying, 'Let's get this guy a baby.'"

Gaby smiled and then laughed.

The New York Fertility Center was well known and recommended by a colleague, Kyle, a cocky oral surgeon who had an office in my building. He and his wife had recently had twins.

"I hear you," Kyle commiserated with me over lunch. "We did all that crap, too. Just go see Dr. Sarah Wight, no one else," he said. "She's the best. My wife and I got pregnant after three months."

Sure, it had to work; it was based on real science, right?

I wasn't exactly sure what they were going to do at that first appointment. I imagined a consultation, maybe an exam, and not much more.

I sat in the large, comfortable waiting area, casually reading the *New York Times*. The nurse had called Gaby back about fifteen minutes earlier and whisked her away to some exam room.

I was reading an obituary. I love them. It's like reading the credits below a picture in a high school yearbook. The more credits you have, the more popular you seemed to be. To me, obituaries were your final credits. The dead guy I was reading about had a shitload of them: multiple degrees, five published books, a Pulitzer Prize, a wife—and lastly, children.

I couldn't concentrate. What if something was terribly wrong with my machinery?

My dick had never given me a problem. It had been working fine for years. Dicks don't take kindly to criticism, and they pride themselves on being reliable. *Nothing's wrong with my dick.*

Maybe it was my balls—my sperm factory. But that would be fixable, right? I could handle something awry with my balls. *Just leave my dick out of this.*

"First time?" I heard a voice say.

I looked up from my newspaper and saw a middle-aged man with graying temples seated across from me. I smiled, not entirely sure he was talking to me.

"Your first time here, right?" he repeated.

"Yes," I replied, not sure what difference it made.

"I thought so. You look nervous."

I was nervous but didn't want to talk about it with this stranger. "No, I'm okay," I said.

"This is our fifth visit," he said. "One artificial-insem and two IVFs. Still hopeful, though."

I smiled, not sure how to respond and even less sure of what he'd said exactly, since he had said it so fast.

"Ready for the big jerk?" he added.

"Beg your pardon?" I knew what I *thought* I'd heard, but that couldn't be right. And if I had heard correctly, he couldn't be referring to what I thought he was. Or if he was referring to it, maybe in addition to being infertile, he also had Tourette's syndrome.

"Spank the monkey? Stroke the pickle? Beat the pud?" he said as he did a quick demo with his hand. "For the sperm."

I had heard him correctly.

I was caught off guard. How do you respond when a stranger says something like that to you? *Fuck off!* I remained silent and smiled. It was one of those partial, half grin, half nausea smiles.

"I can see from the look on your face that you haven't done it yet. Well, let me tell you it's the best thing about this place. They put you in this room with porn in the middle of a workday. How cool is that?"

"And why would they do that?" I asked.

"Duh. To check your swimmers," he answered. "To see if they're up to par. They need a sperm count. That's the first thing they get from you."

"Of course. I knew that," I said with confidence. I wasn't completely out of it. I knew they sometimes needed to check the sperm.

But I also thought that was a last resort. Or at least something that was done later. I never really believed anything was wrong with my sperm. I was in classic male, ego-driven denial.

The stranger wouldn't stop. "It's fantastic. Their porn is great! And believe me, I know my porn."

"Well, I don't think I can do that. Not in a doctor's office."

"That's what everyone says. But wait till you see the porn."

"It's not going to happen," I emphasized.

"Mr. King, come with me, please," said a nurse who was standing near the entrance to the treatment rooms.

As I walked toward the nurse, the man in the waiting room gave me a thumbs-up sign followed by a "spank the monkey" gesture. He was laughing to himself.

"Where's my wife?" I asked the nurse as I followed her to another part of the clinic.

"She's fine. You'll both meet with the doctor later. We have to do some tests first."

"Tests? What tests?" I asked as I continued to follow her.

"Blood work, sperm count, things like that."

"My sperm's fine," I blurted out in defense of my boys. *Lady, you insult my sperm, you insult me.*

"Yeah, stud, you and every other man who comes in here," the nurse said sarcastically.

She led me to a room and opened the door.

"The movie selection is under the TV," she informed me. "Sterilization liquid for your hands and penis is on the table with a collecting cup. When you're done, put the cup in the box on the wall and press that buzzer." She pointed to a button on the wall. "Enjoy."

The nurse started to walk away.

"Wait . . . so let me get this straight. You want me to—"

"That's right, do your stuff," she interrupted me. "The same you boys have been doing since the dawn of mankind."

"But I don't think I can."

"Well, it's either this or doing it at home, then racing your ass back over here to give it to me."

"That's inconvenient," I sighed. "All right. I'll try."

"That's the spirit. When you're done, go to Dr. Wight's office. It's down the hall, second door on your left."

"Wait a minute here," I protested. "You're telling me the doctor is waiting in her office for me to finish? That's a lot of extra pressure. I'm not prepared for this."

The nurse looked annoyed.

"Believe me, she's not waiting for you. Just go there when you're done."

"But—" I started to say, but the nurse had already gone. I stood there for a moment, dumbfounded. I looked around. It was definitely a doctor's treatment room: a sink, a table, the usual sterile atmosphere. If the room were a person, it would be boring. The green recliner and small flat-screened TV on top of a nearby cabinet were definitely out of place. The green chair was draped in green disposable paper, similar to the kind of paper they put on restaurant tables to protect them from food stains. I wondered if the matching was intentional. The remote was next to the TV. I opened the cabinet. There were about a dozen DVDs in colorful jackets picturing women who were about to be very naughty.

Some of the titles seemed promising.

"What the heck," I said to myself as I popped one of the DVDs into the player. I ran it for a minute or two. *Not bad.* Then I popped in another. *Better.* I quickly popped in a third. The bored and horny housewife (star of the film), whose husband had just left for work, was into indiscreet gang bangs. Whoever walked in through her front door was fair game. First there was the UPS guy, then the dry-cleaning guy, followed by the mailman. They were all there to give her more than just a delivery. Like any red-blooded man, I found myself engrossed in the film.

The guy in the waiting room was right. This was great! Where did they get this porn? Did the fertility docs have access to porn catalogues that the general public couldn't get? The fertility clinics couldn't afford to mess around. They had to get right down to business. What if some clinics even had live porn stars who jerked you off? Wouldn't that be great? Could they bill your insurance for that, I wondered?

Soon my pants were around my ankles, and the individual packets of cleanser and lubricant were in my hands. I became oblivious to my surroundings. I didn't care if the doctor was waiting. I wouldn't have cared if a gallery of doctors were observing me on the other side of what could be a two-way mirror that hung on the wall. All I cared about was having my turn with the slutty housewife. *Come here, baby!* And it didn't take long before I was ready to make my deposit.

I stopped to grab the collection jar, which in itself was a big distraction. Luckily, I got back on track. I was close now. I held the jar in one hand while I continued jerking off with the other hand. It was hard to do while seated on the lounge chair, so I stood. And this is where it started to get tricky. One hand was moving faster and faster, approaching that *Star Trek*–warp drive masturbating zone where I was about to come, while the other hand was trying to keep the small jar in front of my dick. It was like a horse was trying to have sex with a hummingbird—nearly impossible. If someone had walked into the room at that moment, they would have thought I was performing some pagan ritual involving apoplectic dance.

I tried to place my moving dick all the way into the jar, but my light-speed appendage kept hitting the sides, nearly knocking the jar out of my hand. Too much was going on. I tried to move the jar closer as my dick moved faster. There was no way I could slow down now. There was no "slow-mo" masturbating speed. This wasn't going to work. I panicked. *This is bullshit. They need to invent some kind of fake-vagina collecting jar that you can screw directly onto your dick. Maybe someone already has.*

Then that first, most potent emission shot out like a missile, completely missed the jar, and landed somewhere on the tiled floor. I managed to align the jar closer, and the second emission landed on the lip of the jar and on my hand as I struggled to keep them together. After that, the rest made it inside.

Freaked out, I moved around the room like a penguin with my pants around my ankles, holding my spent penis and trying to maneuver the rim-shot sperm back into the jar. Then I tried to milk my dick to collect any leftover drops. Using the lid, I then scraped whatever I could find back into the jar. I felt like a forensic scientist collecting evidence—in this case, my own sperm.

I looked at what I had, and I'd say I got about 50 percent of the total ejaculate inside the jar. And about 50 percent of that was probably contaminated by touching the lid or outside of the jar. I looked around for that first emission and couldn't find it. I looked all around the floor, under my shoes, but it had disappeared. My sperm had vanished. Maybe it literally hit the fan and disappeared into the ceiling ducts, circulating throughout the office. Everyone could be breathing my sperm. Or maybe the next guy would find it. Maybe he would have the same trouble. Maybe he would think it was his and use it. I could have a kid from all of this and never even know it!

I looked around again. I couldn't be the first guy to have this problem. They didn't exactly give me great instructions. There should have been a demo video first. I mean, really, it's not easy to jerk off into a small container. A bucket, yes. What I really needed was a nurse to hold the jar.

I decided I'd turn in the sperm deposit anyway and hope for the best. Maybe there was enough. Maybe it wasn't all contaminated. I wondered if the nurse was waiting outside the door, or if the doctor was in her office looking at her watch. I'm not sure how long I was in there. I spent at least ten minutes looking for my lost sperm. I took what I had, opened the metal box on the wall, and put the sperm inside. There was another door on the other side of the box. I rang the buzzer for the pickup.

I cleaned the room a bit so it looked normal (just like I did in high school after I masturbated so my mom would not suspect a thing). No one had picked up my deposit yet. I buzzed again. I didn't want to just leave my sperm sitting there. Anyone could take it. Maybe there was a sperm black market out there! There was no response.

"Hello?" I yelled inside the box. "Can you take my sperm, please?" The other door opened and a gloved hand appeared, as if no body were attached, grabbed my sperm out of the box, and disappeared. The small door slammed shut as if the glove were pissed off. It was like a weird puppet act or something out of *The Addams Family* TV show.

I left the room. Thank God no one was waiting. I went to the doctor's office without encountering any snickering nurses along the way.

CHAPTER 11

Sperm and Egg

I DON'T KNOW IF ALL FERTILITY DOCTORS have chalkboards in their consultation office, but ours did. I noticed the board when I shook Dr. Wight's hand. She was a tall, attractive woman in her fifties. She wore a brown suit but no lab coat. She looked more like a Wall Street banker than an MD. My sperm nurse came into the room and handed Dr. Wight a piece of paper. The doctor looked at it for a few seconds and then placed it back on her desk.

Was that about me and my sperm? Already?

Gaby and I watched Dr. Wight draw some pictures on the blackboard of what I suppose were my sperm and Gaby's uterus. I'd seen live sperm before. There was a microscope in my uncle Herman's office. He was a pediatrician. When I went to see him for my ninth-grade physical, no one told me you weren't supposed to wack off the night before your yearly physical exam. In ninth grade, wacking off was pretty much all that I was doing. Who knew that sperm would show up in my urine sample?

"Aren't they cute?" Uncle Herman said as he stepped away from the microscope to give me a look.

I looked through the high-powered eyepieces and knew exactly what I was looking at. They looked like the pictures in my biology textbook: flagella-like organisms scurrying about the slide, bumping into each other with nowhere to go.

I looked at my uncle with great concern.

"Don't worry, I'm not going to tell your mom I saw sperm in your urine," he reassured me. "Next time try not to masturbate before your exam."

Advice I still use to this day.

Dr. Wight's drawing of the sperm on the blackboard looked nothing like the real thing. In fact, if you added legs, they looked like headless mice with long tails. Gaby's uterus looked even worse, like some long-armed alien in a *Men in Black* movie.

Dr. Wight, you need to earn a Drawing 101 certificate to add to all those others on your wall, I thought.

"Now this is a normal uterus, but yours has a slight tilt," Dr. Wight said as she chalked in a uterus at a different angle. "It doesn't mean you can't get pregnant; it just makes it a little more difficult."

Apparently, sperm have trouble making right or left turns and prefer just to go straight. Who knew?

"And the second potential problem is Michael's sperm," Dr. Wight said as she looked deeply into my eyes as if she were a prosecutor trying to crack a defense witness.

"What's wrong with my sperm?" I asked in disbelief. Maybe they just needed a little tune-up.

Dr. Wight, be careful with your words. If you insult my sperm, then you insult my mojo. And nobody, not even a fertility doctor, gets away with insulting my mojo.

She looked at me as if she sensed my hostility building and eased her tone of voice.

"Now this sperm—" she said, pointing to another drawing that was already on the blackboard, "is more regular in shape. But some of yours are like this one." She pointed to the one she had just drawn. "As you can see, it is more irregular in shape."

"You mean like a shirt?" I said, but Dr. Wight didn't look amused.

"No, I mean that their morphology is different," she answered. "They're not as motile as they should be and may have trouble reaching the egg. It happens as you get older."

"But I've got a lot of sperm, right? Millions and billions? They can't all be slow," I objected.

"Of course, there are good ones in the bunch. You are still very capable of getting your wife pregnant."

Hallelujah! Can we stop now and go home? That was the answer I was looking for.

"But if you look at the statistics, here is the percent chance of a female with no issues getting pregnant at forty years old," she said, pointing to some red numbers that seemed to be permanently engraved on the blackboard.

"She's thirty-nine," I interrupted on Gaby's behalf.

"Close enough," Dr. Wight continued. "There's normally about a forty percent chance of getting pregnant, but look how quickly that drops. By forty-three, you only have a one to two percent chance of getting pregnant."

None of that sounded good to me. From the look on Gaby's face, she agreed.

"And then you add the tilted uterus and the percentage falls to here," Dr. Wight said as she pointed to an even lower number on the blackboard. "And the nature of Michael's sperm could lower it to here," she added and pointed to a still lower number.

I looked, but all my brain shut down when she said "Michael's sperm." Why was she addressing my sperm in the third person, as if they were sitting in a chair right next to me, and beside a chair where Gaby's uterus sat?

"From my experience," Dr. Wight continued, "the more aggressively you approach this, the quicker you'll get results—the quicker you will be able to start a family."

Gaby stared at the numbers for a moment. "Well, considering everything, what percentage are we at?" she asked.

"I'd say there is about a ten to twenty percent chance you can get pregnant without intervention. But each year it doesn't happen, the percentage goes down."

Not a good bet for us.

"So how do we improve the odds?" I asked.

"As I've already discussed with your wife, your odds are greatest with IVF, in vitro fertilization. When you factor in everything, it is clear that's the best possible way."

Gaby and I had known that IVF was always an option. We had friends who'd done it successfully. It was proactive, invasive, and not cheap. In fact, anything you do to get pregnant, above and beyond the natural way, is expensive. For most people, the cost of getting pregnant is free. Just follow the basic instructions, insert, and release. So easy. We had moved on to intervention. This was much more complicated, much more involved. But it wasn't the money that gave us pause. It was Gaby's fear.

"Now, as I'm sure you are aware, Gabriella is opposed to IVF. She informed me that she's reluctant to take medication, which makes our job much more difficult."

"I'm sorry, honey," Gaby said as she grabbed my hand. What we had previously discussed in private was now being made public. I felt exposed. I'm sure Gaby did, too.

Gaby knew her fears were irrational, as most fears are. But she hated introducing anything foreign to her body. She was even reluctant to take an ibuprofen. One time she had severe bronchitis, but only when her temperature reached 102 degrees did she agree to take antibiotics. Even then I think she only took them because the high fever was making her hallucinate. She thought her skin was smoking from the heat.

Gaby suspected such fears had something to do with her mom, who had died young, but only after taking many drugs in a failed attempt to get better. To Gaby, drugs meant surrender, giving up control of her body—as if once they were introduced, they would be one of the last barriers to death. She was adamant: no drugs.

But we needed to do something. Time was running out.

"Hey, don't worry, honey—we'll think of something else," I said, grabbing Gaby's hand.

"However, she has agreed to try intrauterine or artificial insemination," Dr. Wight added. "Which requires only some medication."

"Really?" I said, surprised that Gaby would ever agree to that.

"I'm okay with that, honey. Dr. Wight explained everything to me, and I think I can do that."

"That's great!" Knowing her fears, I was amazed that Gaby was on board. Whatever Dr. Wight said to her had worked. If we were going to have a baby, artificial insemination seemed to be as close a substitute as possible to a natural pregnancy.

Dr. Wight was cautious. "As I explained, even though you'll be taking Clomid, AI is not the most reliable solution, but it does work. And certainly, it is better than doing nothing."

Gaby and I looked at each other. It sounded good to us. We thanked Dr. Wight and left the office, confident that we had chosen a good alternative. This was going to work; I felt it in my bones.

I glanced one last time at the blackboard as we walked out of the room. My sperm and my wife's uterus were still up there. Was Dr. Wight going to erase the drawings? Would the next patients see them? Was it legal for the next couple to see illustrations, even bad ones, of our junk on a chalkboard without our permission? I soon forgot about it. We had bigger battles to fight.

CHAPTER 12

Mildly Invasive

Our artificial insemination was scheduled on a Thursday morning. It was a simple procedure, much less invasive than IVF would have been. Gaby reluctantly took the medication to increase her chances of superovulation: dropping more than one egg. The more eggs, the greater the chance that my swimmers would hit something.

The frozen sperm from my initial visit were "washed" in some way that isolated the more potent ones. They were then placed into a syringe and shot into a catheter that extended up into Gaby's uterus toward what we hoped was a traffic jam of eggs. It was an accident we wanted to happen.

My nerdy sperm would head toward a busy intersection of Gaby's attractive eggs, hoping to bump into at least one of them.

Gaby and I felt good about our choice. We kept reminding ourselves that even with all the medical factors lowering our odds of success, the procedure did work. Even the doctor had said it was certainly better than doing nothing. We just needed a little bit of luck. Every pregnancy requires that.

The whole procedure, from prepping Gaby to inserting a syringe filled with my super sperm, took about an hour. We were in and out of the clinic in under two hours. Now all we needed to do was wait.

Calendars are indispensable when you're trying to get pregnant. Even though we were having sex nearly every day, we still tried to figure out the specifics of Gaby's cycle. Like farmers planting seeds for the next growing season, we plotted our implantations. Some women are lucky and can tell when they are about to ovulate. Gaby wasn't one of those. Her cycle varied so much it involved a lot of guesswork.

But with AI it seemed predictable; we knew the egg and the sperm would be on the same page. The guesswork was taken out of it. Twenty-four hours after Gaby was given the Clomid to induce ovulation, the sperm were released.

Luck seemed to be with us; two weeks after the AI, Gaby's period was a day late. We were elated. I wasn't about to hand out cigars yet, but everything looked good. *Mission control, we are good to go* kept ringing in my head.

Two days late: we were feeling even luckier. Gaby felt none of the sluggishness or other signs that she was about to have her period.

Another day passed and still nothing—we were on our way. I hugged her on the evening of the third nonperiod night, confident that we were successful. Our little bambino was in the oven.

On the fourth day, she saw some spotting. We were told that it might not mean anything. Women can spot and still be pregnant. We tried to hold on to our optimism. That was all we could do: think positive.

"It took, honey. I know it," I said.

"You're right. I feel it, too," Gaby agreed.

We hugged in bed that night, thinking somehow our closeness would keep our luck going. She awoke early the next morning and went to the bathroom. I felt her leave the bed. It was rare that either of us had a good night's sleep. The worry and stress of trying to get pregnant took a toll on our bodies and minds, and a good night's sleep was one of the first things to go.

When Gaby returned to the bed, she lay down close to me and buried her head in the pillow. I could hear the muffled sounds of sniffling. I rubbed her back with the palm of my hand.

"Are you okay, honey?" I asked.

"I'm bleeding," she said with barely a whisper.

I just wrapped my arms around her. We were so close. As in a race with a photo finish, you waited for the results, only to find out you had lost. It was hard to hide the disappointment. Even though we'd been through it before—the waiting, the hoping, the wishing—we thought this time it was different. We had moved on to the proactive stage where science intervenes to help nature do its thing, a stage where hope is elevated. So when the intervention didn't work, the disappointment felt even worse.

We avoided the subject of what to do next for a few days. But it was a constant question in our lives, and we knew the sooner we addressed it, the sooner we could move on.

"You know, once is nothing," I said to Gaby at our Saturday lunch. She often waited for me to finish my half-day Saturdays in the office to have lunch with me at our local Le Pain Quotidien.

"I know. People have to do it multiple times. I know all that," she said, looking at her coffee.

"Do you think we should try it again?" I asked. "It's up to you."

Gaby looked into my eyes without saying anything—the kind of look she gave when searching for an answer.

"Just one more," she said.

This was a huge deal for her. The anxiety that *any* intervention produced in her was great. Her willingness to try insemination again really highlighted her desire to have a baby.

I was glad she agreed. I figured another go at it had to increase our chances, just by the law of averages. The more you do something, the more likely you'll succeed, right? Wasn't that what we'd learned? Often the difference between success and failure is perseverance.

Unlike my disastrous first attempt, this one was successful: I managed to collect all the semen. A perfect shot into the plastic jar. Zero spillage. Zero contamination. My sperm were psyched. The magic hand came into the metal collection box and whisked my sample away. I was certain it was going to work this time. The egg had no chance of escaping my giant bolus of premium sperm. I smiled at the same nurse as we left the clinic, giving her the thumbs-up sign. She grinned back, but I couldn't tell if she was happy or disgusted.

This time Gaby's period came on the exact day it was due. The disappointment was so much greater. The sadness reached a whole new level because we realized we just couldn't go on with this. Gaby had felt that even minimally invasive AI was doing things to her body that weren't meant to be done. Her philosophy of que será, será was being torn to shreds. We had tried twice and it hadn't worked. Enough was enough and I knew it. I had promised I wouldn't ask her to compromise again.

But the discouragement was hard to buck, especially for Gaby. Now it seemed that all we had left was luck. Maybe it hadn't completely abandoned us. Maybe we could still be an exception to the rule. We could only hope.

"We can still have a child, you know," I said. It was a few days after the ill-fated second insemination. "The doctor said you could still get pregnant."

"I know," Gaby said. The soft surrendering tone of her voice reflected the impact not only of turning forty but of being childless.

"Just look on the Internet: tons and tons of women over forty still get pregnant. It happens."

Gaby smiled. "I know that, sweetie." She touched my cheek as if she hoped some of my optimism would rub off on her. But it didn't.

The harder and longer we tried to have a child, the more we wanted one. It overshadowed everything we did. We couldn't look at other children the same. We saw them, touched them, hugged or kissed them, but still they weren't ours. And it hurt deep inside that they were not, so much that our burning desire to be parents turned us cold to the idea. It was the only way we could cope. We became numb. We became victims. We had to change our stance on the importance of having a child. Optimism, pessimism, apathy, all the ups and the downs—we just couldn't do it anymore. It was too painful. We had to protect ourselves, to distance ourselves from it all.

So gradually we placed getting pregnant on the back burner with an out-of-sight, out-of-mind resignation. We rarely talked about it. We focused on work, travel, and loving each other, a life without issues. Time made it easier to forget, although we both knew that percolating just below our carefree demeanor lurked the sorrow of uncompleted business. And with that, life moved on.

PART IV

RIDING THE CYCLONE

CHAPTER 13

What Now?

GABY WAS APPROACHING HER MIDFORTIES, and I was approaching the age where the clerk at the movie theater would give me a senior ticket without asking first.

It was a Tuesday night, and Gaby had just gotten home from her weekly tennis match. "Do you still want a child?" she asked as she slipped out of her sneakers.

I wasn't sure why she had suddenly brought it up now. We both seemed to be doing great. My mindset had returned to being married without children. Besides, I was getting too old for all that shit. Still, I knew it was best not to hesitate with my answer. I didn't want to upset her ever again the way I had in the past by not wanting a kid when she did. I loved her too much for that. I'd gotten onboard before, and I could do it again.

"Sure," I said.

"Good. So do I," she said. "We need a plan. Time is running out."

Gaby had been playing a lot of tennis lately—maybe she had gotten hit in the head with a tennis ball! But something had awakened her desire to revisit this. Truth be told, I knew it had always been there, simmering. "Sure" was the green light she needed.

"Let's weigh our options. Do your list thing," Gaby ordered.

I prided myself on having read a couple of books to help with my decision-making process, and lists were an essential part. I first wrote down my options. Then I wrote all the pros and cons for each option. I saw more clearly what I could or couldn't live without. Compromise was an essential part of making the most practical decision.

Gaby hated what she called my "*fooking* lists." They weren't very French. She could decide just with her gut. And I was sure she had already made a decision. Still, she knew I needed the math-major, male-logic clarity that lists provided, and so she indulged me.

"Just to be fair," I said over dinner, "I'm including all options."

"Go ahead," Gaby said as if it didn't matter.

And I knew it didn't. *Why play this fucking game? Just ask her what she wants,* I thought. But I went ahead anyway.

1. *Forget about it.* Even though I had told her "Sure," I left this option as a possibility. "Happy couples without kids are happier than happy couples with kids," my sister Andie had once told me. Apparently there was a study out there that confirmed that. It sounded reasonable.

2. *Do nothing and hope.* Women do get pregnant at forty-four. It happened. Although in reality the chances were low, under 1 percent, miracles did sometimes happen.

3. *Try surrogacy.* Use Gaby's eggs and my sperm, but just let somebody else do the work of carrying the child to term. It was IVF with a stranger's uterus, a stranger usually recruited by an agency. The surrogate moms were young, and many already had a child or two, so the chances of their carrying a baby to term were high. Surrogacy had the best odds in our favor.

4. *Adopt.* People did it every day. I'd seen plenty of adopted kids in my practice, and they were great, with parents who loved them no differently than they would their biological child.

5. *Find a child through the unscrupulous dark web.* I'd heard of it but didn't have any idea whether the rumors I'd heard were true.

I showed Gaby my list as I continued with the charade.

She took a red pen and started making an *X* through each option as she read it.

"No," she said as she crossed off option one. "No, this one is almost like the first one," she said as she read options two and three. "No, and definitely no."

"What?" I said as I grabbed the list. "We didn't even discuss them."

"I don't have to."

"I do. That's the purpose of lists."

"Your lists, not mine!" Gaby replied.

I looked at option one with its big red *X.* "But you love our freedom to travel so much," I said, reinforcing my case for keeping the status quo. "You told me so yourself."

"I do love it," Gaby agreed. "But we can still travel with a kid—maybe not as much, but we can still go places."

"You're right. But, you know, happy couples without kids are happier than happy couples with kids," I added.

"Your sister told me that," Gaby said. "You don't really believe that, do you?"

Warning: give her the answer she's looking for, not yours.

I had this 75 percent theory. Yes, another fucking theory. If you got along with your significant other at least 75 percent of the time, that made for a successful relationship. The 75 percenters, I reasoned, bickered, but not that much. They had their differences like any couple, but they never went to bed angry. They didn't stop talking to each other for hours or days. They always respected the other's opinion. And most of all, the 75 percenters never tried to change or mold the other person but accepted them as they were. My theory sounded good, but I think it just boiled down to this: 75 percent of the time they agreed that the wife was right.

"Of course not," I replied. "We'll be just as happy with a kid."

I looked at option two, "Do nothing and hope," which she had crossed off, although with a smaller *X*. Gaby was right; it was too similar to option one. I'd better forget about option two.

All right, I surrender. Stop this game.

"You're right. With these options, we're still not certain we'll ever have a family," I said.

"How come you know me so well?" Gaby asked with a smile.

"Hey, ten years together, I was bound to pick up something," I said, and smiled back.

"How about a dog instead of a kid?" I added as a joke.

"You know that's not the same thing at all," Gaby answered.

When we were having trouble getting pregnant, we'd talked about getting a dog. Maybe a canine would make up for not having a child. But neither of us wanted to be one of those pet couples. What is it with childless married people who whip out pictures of their dogs? And what are we supposed to say? "He's so cute. He looks just like you. He has your eyes."

I love pets. I grew up with dogs. They provide comfort and in some cases are better companions than humans. They counteract loneliness for many. I get all that. But Gaby and I had made a pact that if either of us showed off a picture of our "Coco," or whatever eventual pet, the other person was allowed to murder them. For us a family consisted of at least three, and pets didn't count.

"I see finding a kid on the dark web is out. Why?" I asked, skipping a couple of options and trying to change the mood.

Gaby shook her head. "Give me a brick. It's not funny."

"That's 'break,' honey—'give me a break.'"

Sometimes I think the only difference between being funny or not is how many jokes you try. It's akin to the professional photographer who takes a thousand pictures in order to get one great shot. The more jokes you make, the greater the chance that at least one of them will be funny. Gaby was right, it wasn't funny, and for that one I really did deserve a brick in the head.

That left us with surrogacy and adoption. She had started to cross out surrogacy when I grabbed the list from her.

I liked the idea. It would be our biological child. We could see what our genes were capable of producing, so that long after I was gone someone would look just like me. How cool would that be? That option was a slam-dunk for me. It was my number-one choice. Plus, it had a high rate of success.

"I know we talked about surrogacy before," I said. "But I still think it's a great option."

"Absolutely not," Gaby replied.

"We don't have to use your egg," I said. "Aren't half our genes better than none at all?"

The look in Gaby's eyes was demonic.

Did I fucking just say that? Can I take it back? A do-over?

I knew she hated the idea of surrogacy. Gaby had set boundaries, and surrogacy somehow stepped over the line. With so many unwanted kids in the world, it felt inherently wrong to her to have to go to such extreme measures to get a child. Still, I thought I'd give it another try.

"You're right," I said in panic mode as I tried to dig myself out of a hole before she could say words that matched her knifelike stare. "I'm sorry I even brought it up."

She relaxed a bit, and I was thankful I was still alive.

I'd talked with other men about the mental games we played with our wives. It all started out with a disagreement. We stated our case. It sounded logical and we knew that it would hold up in a court of law. But we were idiots to even think that. Facts and logic had nothing to do with conflict resolution in a marriage. Wives allowed us to posture, to do the man thing. I wondered if women enjoyed watching us make fools of ourselves. Then with just a word, a gesture, or a stare from them connoting death and destruction, we surrendered and took the path of least resistance. And the quicker we surrendered, the easier life became.

I should have learned my lesson by now.

I took Gaby's red pen and boldly circled "Option four, adopt." I gave her back the list.

"Really? Really!" Gaby said, almost making me believe it was my idea. She threw her arms around me and held me tight for several seconds. It felt as good as if I had made the decision myself.

Happy wife, happy life.

CHAPTER 14

The Adoption Game

IT WAS A RAINY FRIDAY NIGHT WHEN WE ENTERED a church on the Upper West Side of Manhattan. We worked our way down the long, wide corridor to the room where the lecture was taking place, our footsteps echoing off the old stone floor.

"We're twenty minutes late," Gaby said in a loud whisper.

"It's not my fault there was traffic," I said in my defense.

"It's New York City. There's always traffic," Gaby retaliated. "You knew we didn't give ourselves enough time to get here. You're doing that aggression-passion thing again."

"Honey, it's 'passive-aggressive.'"

"I don't care what you call it. If you don't want to do this, let's leave now."

"I *do* want to do this," I answered, but Gaby could sense my trepidation. It was one thing to talk about adopting, but another matter to actually start the process. It wasn't just talk anymore.

The woman seated at the folding table at the entrance of the room had a sign on her table that read LOVING CHILDREN ADOPTION SEMINAR. I knew there were lots of agencies out there, but this particular agency came highly recommended by Chris, the adoring mom of a very bright and beautiful adopted Asian girl who was a patient of mine.

The woman greeted us with a big smile even though she must have heard our quibbling. "It's okay—you didn't miss much," she said in the calm tone of someone who had probably dealt with a lot of anxious prospective parents.

She was just the kind of woman you would want on your side when considering adoption—one with lots of patience. I thought that was a good sign as she handed us a pamphlet and a handout covering the night's topics.

"Here you are, and please, go right in," she said.

"Thank you," Gaby whispered as she took the syllabus.

We walked into a room filled with people seated on rows of folding chairs. We settled into seats in the last row, and Gaby pointed to the first topic on the sheet: "Is adoption for me?"

A middle-aged woman in a red sweater and charcoal skirt was addressing the crowd. "As I said, I can't give you all the details." Her voice was very clear and her tone precise. "But I will tell you this," she continued. "For those of us who have gone through the process—and I've done it three times myself—it is the most rewarding, gratifying, loving thing we have ever done. And every parent we have dealt with, without exception, feels the same way. All couples will tell you the same thing: once they have their child, it is by far the best thing that ever happened to them."

A nicely dressed woman in front of us had held her hand up since we walked into the room. I'd hated those hand-raising types in high school and college.

"Yes?" the speaker said at last, pointing to the frenetic Hand Raiser.

Hand Raiser quickly dropped her exhausted arm. "It says the cost ranges from $20,000 to over $50,000. Isn't that a big range?"

Of course it is, you idiot.

"Yes, I was going to cover that shortly," the speaker explained with a touch of annoyance. "But briefly, it depends on the current state of the country that you are seeking to adopt from. The ranges are averages. Currently China and Guatemala are open. Guatemala is closer to the lower range, while China is higher. Often the variation is due to things like distance, the number of trips needed to that country, and so on."

I read somewhere that unless you were talking about sex or sports, men could easily become distracted. I don't think I was quite that bad. But when I started to hear the numbers and data that went on and on, all my mind heard was, "Blah, blah, blah, blah." As a further distraction, I started thumbing through the pamphlet and discovered something I needed clarification on, like now. I shot my arm in the air just as urgently as the annoying Hand Raiser.

"Yes, sir?" the speaker said.

"It says here that the combined ages of the parents usually cannot exceed one hundred years. Could you please elaborate on that?" I asked, looking around.

What the hell was this all about? Under normal circumstances, I would be one of the older potential fathers in the room. But this was the reality of New York City, where an abundance of well-off older men were looking to start a first or second family with a younger woman. (Remember my formula: for every year older the man is than his younger wife, he's got to have another $50,000 of net worth.) A few of the men looked like they were old enough to be *my* father. I did at times feel that I was too old to become a dad. But I knew most of that was just an excuse for a deeper fear of being a father. It was okay for me to say I was too old, but not for some fucking bureaucrat to say it: that pissed me off.

"I was going to get to that," the speaker said. "Certain countries have set age limits. It has nothing to do, of course, with your ability to be good parents, but more as a way to cut down on the adoption requests, which for some countries can be overwhelming."

"So, you mean two fifty-year-olds couldn't adopt?" I asked.

Gaby looked at me as if I had announced that she was fifty to a room filled with strangers. She didn't look happy.

Oops, fucked up again.

"Not that my wife is anywhere near fifty. No. She's a million light-years away from fifty." The entire room laughed. I wasn't trying to be funny.

"Yes, it would be more difficult for people whose combined ages are over a hundred to adopt in certain countries," the lecturer answered, but I wasn't satisfied with her reply.

"So let me get this straight," I continued. "A twenty-two-year-old woman and a seventy-seven-year-old man could technically adopt?" *Again, you idiot!* "Or a seventy-seven-year-old woman and a twenty-year-old man?" I quickly added.

I wasn't going for laughs (which I got), so much as I was pointing to the absurdity of such a rule. I hated rules. For every rule, there usually is an exception, so by their very nature rules are flawed.

"I know it makes no sense," the lecturer said with a smile. "We have no control over what other countries require, but I'll go into more detail about that later on. I know you all have a lot of questions. I must ask you to hold them until the end. We have a lot of material to cover, and hopefully we will cover most of what you want to know. Now back to . . . ," she said, but I didn't listen to the rest.

I had been to other countries and experienced foreign bureaucracy. Just getting the simplest of things done could be a pain in the ass. The age thing just added a kink to the whole process. Under the best of circumstances, foreign adoptions took time. Even children who needed to be adopted urgently, who needed a family right away, had to wait for the wheels of bureaucracy to turn first. It didn't seem fair.

The reception that followed the talk was even more informative. We spoke to parents who had been through the process once and wanted to do it again, and others who had done it multiple times. Most others were like us, new to it all.

One very nice woman showed us a picture of her adorable little girl, age two, originally from China.

"She really wants a little sister," the forty-something-year-old mom explained. "It took us nearly two years before Kelsey was ours. We're going for the same orphanage, so hopefully it will expedite things."

From what we gathered, two years was the average length of time it took to adopt a child, but it could take even longer. Plus, you had to factor in all the politics of the country, which could change at any moment.

The forms were another matter. You had to meet all the adoption requirements not only of the state you lived in but of the adoptive country as well. Just the thought of it was overwhelming. It sounded like a lot of homework, and I never liked homework—even if you did get a kid instead of a grade when you finished.

It quickly became apparent to us that people who adopted talked about their kids no differently than other parents. I knew it was naive to think the bond between parents and their biological children was stronger. Still, the idea was hard to escape. In the movies, I saw it all the time, where some bastard pauper had the genes of the dying king. Since the pauper was the real son, his magical genes would enable him to lead the uprising, rescue his father from the evil usurper, and become a benevolent ruler. All bullshit, but it made for a good story. Still, it was nice to hear firsthand how the genetic component had nothing to do with emotions. The love that parents feel for their child is the same whether the child is adopted or biological.

Parents who were raising both adopted and biological children were even more emphatic about the lack of a genetic love link. That night a man named Harold summed it up best. He was about my age, and he and his wife were planning for their second adoption. They also had two of their own biological children in high school. "We love them all the same. As far as how they turn out, it's a crapshoot no matter where they come from."

I thought about it. That pretty much summed up life in general. Sometimes you do everything right and it turns out wrong, and sometimes it's the opposite. Whether it's marriage, what your children become, or what you become, it all requires a little luck. You roll the dice and hope for the best.

CHAPTER 15

Drowning in Lake Adoption

GABY WAS SOLD ON ADOPTING. I wasn't surprised. She told me she pictured a helpless child in a cold orphanage in some Third World country. She would look into those sad eyes and they would suddenly come alive with a look that said, "Mama." It fit nicely into Gaby's nonsurrogacy, give-a-home-to-an-unwanted-child sense of altruism. She admired people who rescued children from that scenario and gave them a loving home.

But that was the romanticized version of adoption. We learned that it was rarely the case. What usually happened was that the orphanage selected a child for you. They sent you pictures. You traveled to meet the child. You would visit the orphanage every day for a week or two in order to establish a relationship with that child. Then, at a later date, you would get the call to come pick up your child.

On the cab ride home from the seminar, Gaby was very quiet.

"What did you think?" I asked.

"They were very organized. But so much reddish tape."

"I agree, very reddish. But you know there is surro—"

"Don't even say it," Gaby interrupted me.

"I talked to the gay friends of the Ettingers," I said.

"Why did you do that? I told you I wasn't interested in surrogacy," Gaby said, very annoyed.

"I know. But just in case. I didn't think it would hurt." I didn't add anything else; I knew better. I just waited, hoping she'd take the bait.

"What did they say?" Gaby asked. I knew she was indulging me.

"They have twins. Apparently that's not uncommon. I talked to Leonard, the dad with red hair. Anyway, he couldn't have been more encouraging. Their children were born a year and a half after the surrogate process started. They even used a donor egg so that the surrogate would have no legal claim to the child. I didn't ask whose sperm it was or if they mixed theirs together. They can do that. I think it's called a swirl."

I waited. Gaby didn't answer so I continued.

"Well, other than the expense, they said they couldn't be happier and would highly recommend it. The child is yours. All tidy without all that other crap involved in the adoption process. They even gave me the names of two great agencies that do most of the work for you."

The cab stopped in front of our apartment. Gaby, without saying a word, got out. I paid the driver and met her at the elevator. She walked into it and pushed the button for our floor. She didn't even look at me; she just stared straight ahead.

I'm really fucked, aren't I? Me and my big mouth.

The elevator stopped on the fifth floor. Gaby quickly got out and went into the apartment without me. I knew I had gone too far. I had tried one last time to go another route, but I'd failed miserably.

I waited a few minutes before I walked into the bedroom. Gaby was sitting on the bed, reading. It was her way of relieving tension, to escape from all that we were going through. I looked at the title of the book she was reading. It was in French.

"Great book. I loved it," I said, hoping she would at least smile. She ignored me. Her eyes remained fixed on the pages of the book.

I sat next to her on the bed. "I'm sorry I brought it up again. I'm just nervous about adoption." There seemed to be too many things out of our control.

"Don't you think I am nervous, too?" Gaby replied.

"I know you are. None of this is easy," I said. But we were out of options. If we were going to be parents, adoption was it, our last resort.

"You're right," I added. "Let's adopt."

"You mean it?" Gaby asked.

"Yes," I said, and she hugged me. "But I think a domestic adoption is safer for us," I elaborated. "That age requirement really gets me nervous."

"Yes, honey, domestic is fine," Gaby said, barely able to contain her excitement. "I already got the name of an adoption attorney. I'll call her tomorrow."

"Great," I said.

Tomorrow? I was going for maybe next month or next year.

I thought we could ease into it, slowly adjust to the idea. I could feel myself start to perspire. We had gone through so much in the past—the pills, the constant sex, the ups and downs, the shrink, the acupuncturist, the artificial inseminations, the lists, the adoption seminar. Now there would be no more delays. We were calling the adoption lawyer.

Even though I believed I wanted this, I didn't know if I was ready for it to start tomorrow.

CHAPTER 16

And Here's How You Play

THREE DAYS AFTER THE SEMINAR, I GOT out of work early and we drove to Tarrytown, New York, to meet Stacy, the adoption attorney. She had been recommended by Gaby's coworker, who said that Stacy had a reputation for being one of New York's best adoption lawyers.

Our meeting was at five o'clock, and we arrived early. Gaby greeted the receptionist like she had arrived for a dream job interview—a job she wanted so badly that she would go out of her way to make a great impression.

As we sat in the waiting room, I watched Gaby. She looked exhilarated, like something great was about to happen. It amplified her natural beauty. Her beatific aura was almost palpable. I was sure that my aura radiated tension and fear. I clenched my teeth.

"Ms. Fein will see you now," the receptionist said.

As we walked into the attorney's office, I had the same feeling as when I'd walked into the treatment room in my gastroenterologist's office a few months earlier to get my colonoscopy. I was really nervous about a probe snaking up my ass, but it turned out it wasn't nearly as bad as my anticipation of it.

"I'm so glad to meet you both," Stacy said as she stood and offered her hand. She was wearing a dark-striped business suit. We exchanged niceties, then sat in the chairs in front of her desk.

"Let me start by giving you a brief summary of what will be required from both of you," she began. She laid down the fundamentals of the adoption process: the home study, the tax returns, the references, the adoption album, the fingerprinting, the FBI check, and on and on. All that was just for the state approval that would allow you to adopt, a necessity before the process could begin in earnest.

The list of things required seemed endless, a huge pain in the ass. For Gaby, the lists were inconsequential, totally meaningless compared to the bigger purpose, the bigger picture.

As Stacy spoke, my mind began to wander.

This is a nice office. I like that painting on the wall. Gaby looks very sexy. I wonder how much Stacy's charging us so far. I wonder if she knows I'm not listening.

Too much was going on all around me. Maybe it was my way of escaping the reality of our situation. Not listening allowed me to remove myself from it all. But how long could I do that? I needed to pay attention.

Concentrate. Fucking concentrate! I screamed in my mind as I forced myself back into the present moment.

"Has either of you ever been arrested?" Stacy asked.

"No, of course not. Right?" Gaby answered looking at me.

"Uh." I abruptly returned to reality and began to think about the question.

Never. Well, once—almost.

I was ten years old and had gotten caught trying to shoot ducks with a friend's Daisy pump-action BB gun near Sloan's Lake. Shooting ducks wasn't allowed in Denver city parks. Who knew?

"I'm just giving you boys a warning this time," the burly policeman who caught us said as he filled out the report. "But if I catch you trying something like this again, I will arrest you. Is that clear?"

"Michael," Gaby said. "Have you ever been arrested?"

"No," I answered. "Never." *No one keeps a report like that.*

"Do you want to go private or through an adoption agency?" Stacy continued as she made notes. She explained the differences. "With an agency, they will decide what child is suitable for you. With a private adoption, you decide."

"Private," we said together before Stacy could say anything else.

"That's what I would recommend, especially because of your age," Stacy said, looking only at me.

Again with the age thing. I was in good health, and in much better shape than most of my friends. *Give me a fucking break. I'm not that old. Enough!*

"Still, you will have to compete with other couples looking for a child as well."

"We are aware of that," Gaby said.

"Of course, if you wanted an older child rather than a newborn, or maybe one with special needs, it would be much easier. You would have many more choices that way."

"We talked about that," Gaby said, smiling at me. "Maybe for our second child, but for the first we'd prefer a newborn who's healthy."

A second child? Let's get the first one and then we'll talk.

"That's what most people want and we try for that," Stacy said, then added, "but we do often have to compromise."

Her many questions spun around in my brain. "Do you have any objections if the child is black, Hispanic, Asian, or biracial? Do you have a sex preference, male or female? Do you want an open adoption, where the child has contact with the birth mother, or a closed adoption, where the child does not?"

It was hard enough for me to choose between chunky or creamy peanut butter. My mind was bombarded with all the information to process and the decisions that needed to be made. A floating diagram appeared in my mind with arrows and lines connecting all the choices, possibilities, and outcomes. It seemed endless, overwhelming in its complexity. It made me dizzy. I was so stressed that I needed a time-out.

Of course we wanted a newborn from a drug-free, psychologically stable birth mom. The choice was clear. But I was naive to think we even had a choice. I was about to learn that even in the best of circumstances the process was filled with uncertainties, with near hits and misses. In the end there was really only one choice: should we take a chance or not?

"I know this is a lot of information to take in," Stacy said.

You think?

"But you don't have to decide now. You can think about what you want to do."

Okay, let's go home.

Stacy must have seen the look of dismay on my face.

I was okay with deciding later, much later. Stacy was right, there was an awful lot of information to digest, and that could take weeks, months, or more. Later was fine by me.

"Well, I like you," Gaby said to Stacy. "And you really were thorough in your presentation. I don't think we need to wait. We're ready. We've been ready. Right, honey?"

Gaby turned and looked deep into my eyes. I could tell there would be no more stalling; she needed to move forward. *Right, honey?* echoed in my head. I was incapable of doing anything except nod my head in agreement.

Writing the retainer check, I had to concentrate to keep my hand from shaking. Not because of the amount, but because of the immense commitment attached to the check. In my mind, I saw a giant wrecking ball at the top of its arc, on its way down toward a peaceful, happy little building soon to be demolished.

We hadn't even left the adoption attorney's office and I was overwhelmed by the process.

I handed Stacy the check, and she handed us a folder packed with papers that needed to be filled out—our homework assignment.

"Is this for our term paper?" I asked. "Term," I repeated, but nobody laughed at the pun. I topped it off with a question that I had been avoiding asking.

"Once all the paperwork and approvals are complete, how long does it take to get it?"

"It?" Stacy asked.

"Sorry, I mean a child," I said. "I didn't really mean anything by 'it.' I'm new at all this."

Gaby shook her head, not believing I had really said that. What I really wanted to ask was if there was some kind of guarantee. *If we do x, y, and z, will we get a child?* Maybe that sounds a little cold, too businesslike when another human being is involved. But we were putting up a lot of money, and I wanted to know what our chances would be for a successful adoption.

"Well, of course there are no guarantees," Stacy said. "I've had clients who got lucky and got their baby in two weeks. Others can take two years or more. It depends on so many factors. Luck is one of them."

I didn't care about the factors. The words "two weeks" kept flashing through my rattled brain like a mantra. Two weeks—two fucking weeks. In two weeks I was planning on ordering a new car. In two weeks so much was going on. I had a life. How could we even make plans if a baby was on the way? How could I be a dad in two weeks? I felt nauseated. I burped, but there was no vomit.

"Sorry," I said, and tried to smile.

CHAPTER 17

I Hate Homework

As we drove home from Stacy's office, I asked Gaby to repeat all the things my distracted mind had barely heard. She was used to it.

"You sure you don't have that A, D, and D thing?" she had asked me more than once. It seemed that many of the kids I grew up with had it: a distraction complex. We had trouble paying attention, perhaps due to an overdose of *I Dream of Jeannie, Gilligan's Island,* and *Bewitched.* We were always distracted unless we were talking about girls and sex. (For those topics, we were always present. If we had an attention deficit, it was selective.)

"Now explain to me again what the adoption facilitator is?" I asked, confused.

"She's the one who puts the ads in the newspapers, fields the phone calls, screens the birth mothers, and then puts us in touch with the ones who fit into our parameters."

"Where does she run these ads?" I asked.

"In markets where there are more pregnant women who may not want to keep their child."

"You mean like the *New York Times*?"

It's amazing how my wife can call me stupid with just her eyes. "No. Like those penny savers we see in the country," Gaby answered.

I knew about penny savers: small suburban-market papers that advertised all kinds of local services and things for sale, like used furniture and other assorted junk. Gaby loved yard sales, estate sales, and vintage sales. She liked things that had a bit of wear on them. She thought it gave them character. Shit, maybe that's why she was attracted to me. Maybe she wanted an older guy with a little rust around the edges, whose tires were slightly balding. I was her vintage husband.

For me it was the opposite. I liked things new. Gaby once tried to buy me a vintage bowling shirt, but I didn't want it. It felt creepy to me. Maybe I'd feel differently if I knew who owned it. But I wasn't about to wear a shirt that some unknown dead guy had worn.

"So, you're telling me we'll find a kid in a penny saver? Don't they sell mostly junk and used shit?"

"You're thick. Do you know that?" Gaby replied. "It's not the kid. It's that the birth moms hopefully read those papers."

"But we don't advertise until we get state approval, right?"

"Right," Gaby answered with an exasperated sigh.

I felt a little relieved. All that other stuff would take months, maybe years, to get through—far more than two weeks.

I needed time to ease into it mentally. In a year or two I'd probably be ready for the penny savers. Gaby would be thorough and would make sure everything was complete. That could take a while.

"Here's the schedule," Gaby said over breakfast the next morning as she handed me some papers. "You can take care of the left side. I'll take care of the right side. I think we can have everything ready for submission in two weeks—three, tops. Stacy says state approval can take as long as six weeks or more depending how many cases they have pending. So we want to get this finished as soon as possible. Oh, and by the way, I canceled our trip to Argentina. I hope you don't mind."

Crap! I was speechless.

"And don't worry, I already contacted the first social worker on our list for the home study, and guess what? She had a cancellation and she's coming over tomorrow!"

"That's so great," I said. There was nowhere to escape, except in my mind.

In the next few hours, Gaby overprepared our apartment for the home-study visit. I didn't see what all the fuss was about.

"They're not going to be that picky," I said. "They just don't want to see a lot of whips, bottles of liquor, or a gun case with loaded weapons. And cocaine. They definitely don't want to see cocaine lying around."

Gaby didn't look happy. "This is not a *fooking* joke. I'm tired of you making everything so light."

"It's 'making light of' everything. But you're right, honey. I'm sorry."

"You can be a real *schmook* sometimes."

"I know. It's just that things are happening so fast."

Gaby smiled. "But just think. It will all be worth it. We'll soon have our baby."

"I know. That's all I think about."

We hugged. I knew her eyes were closed. Out of fear, mine were wide open.

Dr. Dora Rosen was the director of sociology at New York University. We picked her because she was the first name on the list of licensed New York State home-visit evaluators that Stacy had given us. And she was available.

Dora was in her early fifties. She seemed assertive and to the point. She sat on our living-room couch as she asked questions, jotted down notes, and then got right to it.

"Can I see the rest?" Dora asked.

"Sure," Gaby answered, and stood for the tour.

We showed Dora around our apartment. Well, Gaby did the showing. I just followed at a safe distance.

Our two-bedroom, two-and-a-half-bath apartment was rather spacious by New York City standards. The building was prewar and had a doorman, both pluses for any New Yorker. It was clean and uncluttered with a homey feel to it. We had beautiful area rugs and solid, custom-made wood furniture. We liked things simple and made to last. Our compact second bedroom Gaby had designated as the baby's room. It had a whimsical Xavier Cugat oil painting of a circus caravan on the wall.

"Do you have help in taking care of your home?" Dora asked when we returned to the living room. She was looking at Gaby as if I weren't there. I thought that was a weird question. If you knew you were going to have a home study, wouldn't you tidy up?

We are slobs and we'd like our child to grow up to be a slob, too.

Was Dora implying that our apartment was too neat? That we were incapable of doing it ourselves? I kept my mouth shut. But she wasn't blind. She had to make some inferences. All you had to do was look at Gaby to tell she liked things orderly. She was impeccably stylish. Richard described her as "classy as hell," like a young Susan Sarandon. And there was a definite resemblance.

My comedic mind realized how much power I had, and that I could undermine the whole process, or any process for that matter. Any situation can be altered just by doing something weird. What if I picked my nose and rubbed the booger on the couch? That would have to be a deal breaker, even if everything else was perfect, right? And wouldn't Dora have to write that down as the reason we weren't approved? "Nose picker." No one likes nose pickers. They're disgusting. You can't adopt if you're a nose picker. Did I secretly want to do that? Of course not. Or did I? *Go on, pick a booger out. I dare you.* I sat on my hands so I wouldn't be tempted.

"Yes, we do," Gaby replied. "Susie comes in once a week to do housecleaning and laundry."

"I see," Dora said, and jotted down more notes.

What the fuck does that mean?

"We also have a country house," Gaby said.

Dora seemed to lighten up when we told her about the country house. Country houses were good for city kids to get away to on weekends and holidays. Dora also looked at the pictures on the mantel above the fireplace. We always had family pictures, mostly my family since it was much larger. But we brought out even more for the home study: my idea.

I knew I was being passive-aggressive about the adoption, at least in my mind. Even though my actions expressed my desire to adopt, the closer we got to it, the more I realized how life-changing it would be. That was frightening to me.

Dora's whole visit took about an hour, and by the time she left, she knew way too much about us, from how much we made to what kind of car we drove. I wondered how she would rate us. Was there a letter system like they have for New York restaurants? An "A" rating meant no mice or rat droppings, therefore a safe and clean place to raise a child. A "D" rating meant rodents and cockroaches vacation there, so an unsafe place for children. Maybe there should be a rating system for people, too. "Thinking of having a kid? Get rated first!" If it were part of foreplay, it might cut down on unwanted pregnancies or bad parenting. "I want you, I need you, I want your baby—but first, what's your rating?"

Gaby was uneasy about the whole thing. "What if there was something she didn't like?"

"Don't be ridiculous," I said. "What's not to like? We have a great place. We're great people. Aren't we?"

"Yes," Gaby agreed. "But I think you could have talked more; you hardly said a thing. You just sat there."

"I was nervous. Besides, you were doing such a great job," I said.

Gaby looked at me like she didn't quite believe me.

Dora did make me nervous. She was hard to read. What if she thought I was an idiot or that I had terrible social skills? With just a stroke of her pen, she could end it all here. Our adoption option would be out the window. We'd be forced to steal a child. We would end up in jail just because we had a cleaning woman on Wednesdays and I thought about picking my nose.

Three days later Stacy got the results of our home study from Dora. We had Stacy on speakerphone. "Well, how did we do?" Gaby asked.

I felt like I was waiting for my DAT (dental aptitude test) results to see if I would go to dental school or be forced to work in my dad's strip club.

"I have to tell you, Dora's tough. But it's the quickest approval we have ever gotten from her. Congratulations!" Stacy said.

Gaby hugged me. "That's so great! Isn't that fantastic?" she said.

"Yes, it is," I agreed. We had passed with flying colors. Of course we did. We were great. We passed. We passed?

Oh, my God, we passed!

Things picked up from there. Everything was moving according to Gaby's plan. We went to get our fingerprints taken the next day at the local police precinct. Appointments were made for our physicals. We were on an express train to Kidsville. A week later, everything was sent off to Stacy, who submitted it to the state of New York for approval.

Then once again, we waited. Adoption seemed to involve a lot of waiting. Nothing was immediate. Meanwhile, it was time to put together our adoption album. This is what the birth mothers look at when they are choosing the adoptive parents. They know there will be a demand for their baby, but they make the final decision—maybe the last one they'll ever get to make when it comes to their child.

The adoption album was essentially a picture scrapbook of Gaby and me doing things.

"Show loving things," Stacy explained, "like hanging out with friends and family, being on vacation, and interacting with children. You need many pictures of you guys with children."

There were adoption-album standards and guidelines, and one article summed it up as follows. "Be sincere, be honest, and always let the birth mother know how grateful you are that she is considering you to be the parents of her child. Pictures of your home and anything else that puts you in a positive light to reassure the birth mother are important. And if she likes what she sees, hopefully you'll make her prospective parents list."

It was a sales pitch for the birth mother, a testimonial in pictures and captions that in the end said, "Please let us love your child as you clearly see we are capable of doing. This is who we are and what we look like. So please choose us." It gave the birth mom a sort of road map of what life would be like with us as parents.

"All this can be really tough for the BM," Stacy divulged through the speakerphone. "She is giving up so much. She just wants to know that her child will be given a better life than she would be able to provide. Love is so important. It's a word you're going to use often. Your album has to ooze love. Most of these mothers have already made the toughest choice they have ever made: to give away their baby. Now they face another tough choice: finding the right home for their child. A stable, loving family is all they want for their child even though their own lives are often falling apart."

So there go the pictures of me walking around the apartment with my underwear on my head.

Gaby was the creative one in the album department. She had studied at the Fashion Institute of Technology. It took her three days to get the album together. She took a few days off from her job and worked on it day and night. She chose pictures from old albums as well as new ones exported from iPhoto. Our album told a story—a love story. There were pictures of the French restaurant where Gaby and I first met, of our wedding, of us on vacation, of us with friends and family, of our apartment in the city and of our country home—even pictures showing the BM where the baby's room would be.

I was proud of our album. Gaby had done an outstanding job. Who in her right mind could refuse a couple like the one in all those photos? "Whoever gets this," I told her, "will want us to be her child's parents."

"You think?" she asked.

"Absolutely. You know, you could do this professionally."

"Really?"

"Yes, it's really incredible how good it is. After looking at it, *I'd* adopt us."

Gaby beamed. She was proud of what she had done.

It was so good, I was sure we'd only need one copy. But Gaby was more in tune with the reality of adoption. We settled on five copies. Five chances that one of the mothers would like us enough to give us her baby. Five chances to become a parent—to become a dad.

It was one o'clock in the morning when I went to Kinko's to make copies. Gaby later collated them and bound them like a book. There was a picture of us on the cover, sitting on a park bench on a beautiful spring day surrounded by trees and flowers in bloom. We were hugging and smiling. It was a picture filled with hope and promise, a picture that said, "We are ready."

CHAPTER 18

Vanishing Moms

THE NEXT PERSON WE MET ON OUR adoption journey was the ominously named facilitator. "Facilitator" sounded to me like Harvey Keitel's character, the fixer, in Quentin Tarantino's film *Pulp Fiction*. The fixer was the guy who made things go away—disposed of the murdered dead body and cleaned up all the mess. Like the fixer, the facilitator cleaned up the mess; but in this case, the mess was all the red tape for adopting a child. Everything was set up and arranged through the facilitator.

Holly Robins came highly recommended by Stacy, and she was selected by our usual scientific method: she was first on Stacy's list of choices. Plus, she had great credentials. She was a licensed attorney with a degree in social work. At a mere $200 an hour, she would place the ads, which we paid for, and then screen the birth moms who responded. After she let us know which ones seemed the most promising, we would call them on our newly acquired 888 phone line. (An 888 number was part of the anonymity factor required for a closed adoption.)

But we still had to wait for state approval before we could move ahead with any of this. We were in adoption limbo.

"We just have to be patient," Stacy said. "It could take weeks or months, depending on how backed up the courts are."

Still, Gaby called every week to see if there was any news. The longer it took, the more Gaby worried.

"What if we don't get approved?" Gaby asked me.

"Are you crazy? Why wouldn't we get approved? We're great. We're smart, we're fun, we live in a great city, we've got a little money. Who would make better parents than we would?"

"You're right," Gaby agreed with a hesitant smile.

After a month had passed, I started to get a little worried, too. No, "worried" was the wrong word—more "insulted." Are they crazy? I hate bureaucracy. Could the state actually be considering denying us an adoption certificate? Was there something we'd overlooked?

But while we waited, I got a reprieve from all the anxiety I was feeling. My confusion—I want to adopt, I don't want, I'm not sure—was exhausting. I welcomed the break and put the whole adoption thing in the back of my mind while I continued to do what I had been doing: working, eating, exercising, performing at a comedy club one or two nights a week, and just hanging out in my sweet status-quo life. It was an easy life to fall back to.

When the five-week mark passed, Gaby was out of sorts. By the sixth week, she was certain we weren't getting approved.

"You're happy, right?" Gaby asked me one morning over breakfast.

"Yes, very happy, honey," I answered, knowing what was next.

"And it's okay with you if we're never parents?"

"Gaby, Stacy said it takes a minimum of four weeks and up to three months to get the approval. I think there are only one or two judges who handle all the cases for the state."

"I know, but still, why would it take so long if everything was fine? You yourself said we have the right stuff or whatever you call it."

Gaby was sure something was up. "I bet it's because I'm French. Americans aren't crazy about the French. They're making this a political issue."

"Don't be ridiculous," I said.

"I should call Stacy again." Gaby went for the phone.

"You just talked to her yesterday and the day before that. She said as soon as she hears from them she'll get back to us. And it's Saturday night. I'm sure she doesn't want to hear from us on a Saturday night."

With that, Gaby put down the phone.

On Tuesday morning, we were getting ready for work when the phone rang. I saw from the caller ID it was Stacy. I answered the phone as Gaby came running out of the bathroom. She was still drying herself with a towel, naked and partially wet. For a moment, I could've cared less what Stacy had to say. *Look at that body!*

Gaby glared at me, having seen that horny look before.

"Now? Really?" she said, and that snapped my mind—and penis—back to reality.

I heard Stacy's voice over the phone: "Hello? Hello?"

Gaby stared at me as I spoke to Stacy.

"Yes. Yes. Yes. Wow. Okay . . . I'll tell her . . . thanks."

Stacy hung up the phone, but I pretended I was still talking to her. "I understand. Okay. Well, maybe next time. Okay. Thank you. Bye." I hung up the phone. I paused for a moment. I was trying to torment Gaby.

"Well, it's very subjective and the courts don't always get it right," I said as I tried to keep a straight face, but I wasn't good at it. I couldn't hold it. I smiled. And in that instant Gaby knew.

"We got it?" she asked, smiling with a little less than 100 percent certainty.

"Of course we did. Honey, didn't I tell you we would? No problem. Stacy said we could start putting the ads in."

She hugged me. "It's happening. It's really happening." Before I could add another word, Gaby had picked up the phone to call Holly Robins.

The Surrogate Court of the State of New York had certified us as qualified adoptive parents. It was good for a year and a half, which should be more than enough time. The cost for the ads was $8,000. That was the royal package that would blanket many potential BM markets: Texas, Louisiana, Oregon, Washington State, Wyoming, Utah, Indiana, and Idaho. And of course, there were the penny savers. The personal ads were always the same.

Adopt

Adoring dentist and creative Internet professional hope to fill your baby's life with fun and laughter. Expenses paid. Michael and Gabriella 1-888-316-8425

It was that simple. The ads would run Wednesday through Sunday for two weeks in each paper.

"The waiting time is less in these eight states," Holly explained. She had been doing this for years. She was a professional. She knew the markets where she'd had good luck with past adoptions.

"That's how long the birth mother has to change her mind. It's a grace period when she can decide if she wants to keep the child. A week is too long. You want the states with five days' waiting time or less. Three days is optimal. That's about the best you can hope for."

"You mean she can take the baby back if she wants?" Gaby asked.

"Yes, sometimes it happens," Holly answered.

"That's horrible," Gaby said.

"Yes, it is," Holly agreed. "But once the three or four days have passed, there's not much she can do. Years ago, it was much worse. Some babies were returned a year or two later. This was before they had laws in place to protect the adoptive parents."

"Thank God for that," Gaby replied.

But as we proceeded I became more anxious. I wasn't thinking like an expectant father; I was still thinking like a reluctant one. My hesitation, no matter how well I hid it, couldn't be good for the whole process. Yet I had just signed a check for $8,000 for ads in papers I had never heard of, in places where I had never been. The images and notions I had about these places weren't pretty. What kind of people lived there? Had they ever seen a Jew or someone French? I was being a mental prick about the whole thing. I had two choices. Either I came to terms with what we were doing and got on board, or I had to come clean about the fact that I couldn't go through with it. One way or another, I couldn't keep up the facade. I decided to tell Gaby I needed more time . . . except that Holly had already placed the ads. She was way too efficient.

Gaby was beyond excited. I decided to keep my mouth shut. It was Saturday morning. I got up early to run, but Gaby was up before I was.

"Didn't Holly say she'd call first and tell us about the birth moms, and then we were to call them?" Gaby was talking to me but more to herself.

She was at the breakfast table, having her morning coffee. Like a politician waiting for important news about a major political event, she stared at the two phones in front of her—our regular landline and the 888 cellphone.

"Yes, honey," I agreed as I started to stretch. "But it's only the first day. Holly said it could take a while. Do you want to come running with me? I think you need to get outside and get your mind off all this."

"You go ahead. I'm fine."

"How about I pick you up a bagel?"

"That would be great, sweetheart."

I kissed her on the head.

"Don't forget we have a three o'clock appointment with the decorator," Gaby reminded me.

"Okay, although I still think it's a little early to think about a nursery."

"I know you do," Gaby said. "But even if we don't know the sex of the baby yet, there are lots of options. We can get the major furniture now and then add the boy or girl touches later on."

"I just don't want you to be too disappointed if it doesn't work out, that's all. I mean, this is just the first round of ads."

"I know. I don't know why, but I just feel good about it," Gaby said. "Everything went so quickly. I just think we're on a great path now."

It's too early. I'm not ready!

I was so thankful she couldn't read my mind. I couldn't say anything. Not now. I needed the right moment—a low. I needed a significant low when Gaby wasn't flying so high.

We bought baby furniture on Saturday and more furniture on Sunday. Still no phone calls from Holly.

"Please call her. Maybe she doesn't have the right number," Gaby said to me with that worried look she had been wearing way too much lately.

"She has all our numbers. She said she would call when she has something. If we don't hear from her by Monday, I'll call."

"Thank you," Gaby said. She was not thrilled but accepted the compromise.

Sunday night came and we went to see the movie *Forgetting Sarah Marshall.* It was a cute romantic comedy that made me forget that we were waiting for the adoption phone call. Still, we each tightly clutched a phone. (I had my phone on vibrate. Gaby's phone was on the loudest ring possible.)

I remember the exact scene from the movie during which I first felt the sensation in my pocket. Jason Segel's character was coming to terms with his true feelings toward a Hawaiian hotel employee played by Mila Kunis. My phone vibrated in a super-deep earthquake-like vibration that I'm sure shook the whole row of seats. It was hard to ignore. Again and again I felt and heard the annoying vibration.

"Well, are you going to answer it?" Gaby asked in a loud whisper.

"It's not on the 888 number," I whispered back. "It's probably just Richard calling to say hi."

"Just see who it is, please!" Gaby said in a loud whisper.

I took the phone out of my pocket and looked. "It's Holly," I whispered to Gaby. "It's probably nothing. I'm sure she just has a question about something. I'll be right back. You just stay and watch the movie."

I walked quickly to the lobby. The phone was still vibrating when I answered it.

"Hi, Holly. No, no problem. We were just at a movie. *Forgetting Sarah Marshall.* Yeah, it's good."

I was relieved that the phone call was just chitchat and probably not important.

"I got a few interesting calls," Holly revealed.

She said a few. Not one or two—a few. That meant at least three, and it had only been a few days since the ads were placed.

"Okay. Let me get Gaby," I turned to go back into the theater—but Gaby, like a stalker, was standing nearly on top of me, so close that she startled me when I turned.

"You better take it," I said as I handed her the phone.

I watched Gaby's changing expressions. She got more excited as the conversation went on.

"Piece of paper and pen!" Gaby ordered, and I scrambled for the pen in my pocket. For paper I had nothing, so I took an unused napkin from the nearby trash container.

Using my back as a writing desk, Gaby wrote down the names and numbers that Holly dictated to her: Danielle, Caitlin, Crystal. The names were made more significant by the deep pressure of the pen on my back. Gaby scribbled quick notes as she listened intently.

"Okay, okay, I will. I'll call you back." Gaby quickly ended the call.

She was excited. "Three! Can you believe it? Three birth mothers called within the last hour. When it rains, it's wet!"

This wasn't the time to correct her.

"Danielle is the only one I should call now," Gaby continued. "Holly will follow up on the others tomorrow."

Gaby took out the special cellphone, the one with the 888 number. After taking a deep breath, Gaby tapped Danielle's number. Before she entered the last digit, Gaby paused and looked at me. It was a "this is finally it" look.

With each new person involved in our adoption process, it seemed things got further and further away from me. Now that a real potential birth mother was in the picture, it seemed I had lost all control. I was afraid of what was on the other end of that phone call—fearful more than ever of the inevitable change and the responsibility of what was to follow.

Like a lawyer prepping a client for the courtroom, Holly had prepped Gaby for the call. Gaby knew what questions to ask and how to respond: to be understanding, grateful, and caring. It was all about helping the BM in any way she could through this often devastating period. Trust and feeling safe were all important to the BM.

I knew Gaby was ready. She had prepared as much as she could to meet the challenges. Still, there were always unknown factors you couldn't control, especially with something like this.

So Gaby hesitated like someone who was about to speak to their doctor, wanting but not quite ready to find out the results of some test. The movie theater vanished around us, and it was just Gaby and me and the phone. Gaby tapped the last digit and then looked into my eyes as she said, "Hello, Danielle."

Those were the first words Gaby said to a birth mother whose baby we might actually adopt. For me, it might as well have been "Houston, we have landed." *Holy shit!*

The anticipation was high. Gaby was speaking to someone who had suddenly taken on an ethereal quality, someone who could have a profound influence on our lives, someone who could give us a child.

"This is Gabriella," she said. "I'm so glad you responded to our ad." She then slowly relaxed into the conversation. We moved to a bench in the theater lobby. Using more napkins, Gaby took notes as she talked and I watched. I felt like I was watching a real-life soap opera unfold right in front of me. I forgot about *Forgetting Sarah Marshall.*

Gaby wasn't doing much talking, just nodding as she repeated, "Yes . . . yes . . . yes . . ."

Too many yeses and noes didn't seem like a good sign. And the conversation lasted less than five minutes. But then again, how long did it take to establish trust? Could a short conversation be enough for some people?

"Yes, I will. Thank you so much. Goodbye." Gaby hung up, then handed me the phone. She looked drained and took a long pause, as if the wind had been knocked out of her.

"She said she's ready for us to take her baby."

"What?" Just like that we got a baby? One phone call and that was *it*? "What does that mean?" I asked.

"Well, she said we sounded like we were the best choice for her baby," Gaby said.

"She's already had it?" I asked.

"No. I don't think so. I guess so. I don't know. I could barely get a word in. She talked so fast. Blah, blah, blah . . . something about the father being an ass of a hole. He wants nothing to do with her or us. He already has one of her babies. He can't afford another . . . and on . . . and on. She wants us to pick up the baby on Sunday when she leaves the hospital."

"It's Friday!" I screamed.

"You don't think I know that? Stacy said sometimes it happens like that," Gaby said. In a flash, she was back on the phone.

Seated in a chair in the theater lobby, I munched popcorn as I watched Gaby strategize with Stacy and then Holly. I felt like I was watching a scene from the crisis center in an action film where Gaby was at the controls, focused, and doing whatever was necessary to resolve the crisis. I felt disconnected from the drama, an observer eating popcorn. My mind raced. *Two days! This is all a fucking joke, right?*

I tried to take it all in as best I could. The day after tomorrow we were supposed to go somewhere . . . some state where our ad had run, to pick up a baby . . . some baby, our baby. That was all we knew. Many of the details were left to Stacy and Holly to sort out. Gaby was coordinating her part, our part. She took speed notes on other discarded napkins, like a football coach frantically mapping out the winning play.

Then, just like that, the conversations ended. Exhausted, as if she had just sprinted a mile uphill, Gaby plopped down next to me. Together, like robots, we munched on the remaining popcorn. She was too overwhelmed for words.

I knew she was ready for this journey. A cartoon bubble caption above her head would have shown a great big *YES!* My bubble caption would have been *Oh . . . fuck!* I couldn't very well tell her now that I couldn't go through with it. She was flying high toward motherhood while I was on the ground, looking for shelter from the plane buzzing above me, ready to drop the baby bomb.

We went to bed that night, my body soaked in sweat from thoughts of what would lie ahead. In the morning, life as I had known it would be over. I just lay there and stared at the ceiling. *I'm having an out-of-body experience. I can see my body lying here. Am I dead?*

Gaby slept peacefully. We were awakened at nine a.m. when the phone rang.

"Hi, Holly," Gaby said as she smiled into the phone. The smile didn't last. "What are you trying to say?"

I listened closely and could pick up some of Holly's words here and there: "Phone disconnected . . . No listing . . . It happens . . . Don't worry, there will be others."

"She could call back," Gaby said, seeking hope.

"I wouldn't count on it," Holly replied.

"Well, let us know if she does. Thank you for letting us know," Gaby said, and hung up the phone.

Fickleness, irrationality, irresponsibility, addictive personality, and so many other negative traits were part of many birth mothers' profiles. Our schooling in adoption had begun. What sounded too good to be true usually was. We needed to move fast without all the facts. All we knew was this: if we didn't make our move, there were many other couples who would. That was part of the adoption game, and we were new players, fresh out of the starting gate.

We were about to learn that adoption was a gamble. You placed one bet, threw the dice, and winner took all. The adoption process wasn't for sissies. Danielle had probably had good intentions (at least after she'd had a few drinks). Perhaps she *was* ready to give up her baby. Holly called her back again and again. There was no answer. There would never be an answer. Danielle had vanished along with her baby, if there ever was one.

Gaby took it hard. Danielle wasn't from our world: a world with integrity and sincerity, a world where Cub Scouts and Brownies still existed. Gaby tried, but she just couldn't understand how someone who sounded so sincere, so ready to give you something so precious, could be so deceptive. Gaby was convinced that based on their one-time conversation, her interview for motherhood, that she had gotten the job. But the birth mother was the boss, and we were fired.

"How could she have said that to me?" Gaby asked, and then mimicked Danielle: "'You sound so nice. I just know that you'll be a great mother for my baby.' Was that all bulls-of-shit? How can people do that? Play with our emotions that way? Maybe it was something I said. Did I say something I shouldn't have?"

It was easier for Gaby to blame herself. It was more rational than the cruel joke that was being played on us.

"Honey, no, no, you were so great," I said, trying to reassure her. "You didn't say or do anything wrong. She was a stranger. Someone you didn't know anything about. She was just fucked up."

Gaby nodded, trying to reassure herself that there was nothing she could have done that would have changed the outcome.

I could see the bigger picture. We were dealing with a wacko. Why would someone respond to an ad with no intention of following through? I felt anger, resentment, loss, and sorrow. We had started playing a game where not everyone played by the rules. Some people cheated, some lied, and some would do and say things for no reason at all—at least no reason that you could understand. What really happened with Danielle we would never know.

I was angry with a woman I had never met. Twelve hours ago, we had never even heard of her. And now she was the Antichrist: Danielle, the woman who took our baby.

Yet it had never been our baby; things had never gotten that far. Still, the mere idea that the baby *could* be ours, that we *might* be parents, had been enough for us to form a visceral attachment to the idea. Once the possibility of a baby was introduced, it was everywhere. A simple yes was all that was needed to start a chain of emotional events. Just like that, it became our baby, in mind and in heart. Even the faintest hope ignited something in us—in me.

Yes, I wanted this baby, too!

Then, just as quickly, that feeling was extinguished. That was what made the whole adoption business so hard. The stakes were so dangerously high.

The pain was most evident in Gaby's eyes. That clear brightness of hope was gone from them.

"It's a process, honey; it takes time," I said. "We knew that. Holly told us that. So did Stacy and the other adoptive parents we've met. If it's not this one, it'll be the next. I feel very good about the next one. It will be the one."

I knew I had hit on the best thing, the only thing, I could have said to her. When she hugged me, I felt the warmth and hope gently come back to her and, for the first time, to me.

And suddenly, just like that, I became an earnest player in the adoption game. I was no longer overwhelmed by a fear of responsibility. I was overwhelmed by something else: the desire to make my wife the happiest woman on the planet. To do whatever it took to secure all the love she deserved—my love and devotion plus the love of a child she so deeply wanted. The checkered flag was lowered, and my journey started for real. I was behind the wheel, driving in a race of indeterminate distance and time—a race where the finish line was hidden in a cloud of uncertainty.

CHAPTER 19

Crapshoot

WE GOT TWENTY MORE CALLS FROM THAT round of ads: a divorced mom from Washington State who didn't know who the father was; a woman in a rehab clinic in Ohio; a nearly homeless woman from Texas; a mother of two who was a recovering alcoholic. Another woman called who was the neighbor of a young couple who were barely out of high school, struggling to get by, and planning to get an abortion. The neighbor was trying to talk them out of it. Two phone calls later the Good Samaritan told us that she had failed.

A sad pregnant woman told us she had one nine-year-old child and that another child had died in an auto accident and she just couldn't handle taking care of a third. Some were past or current drug users or alcoholics. They were married, divorced, separated, or a little of all three. There were even calls from grandparents who were tired of taking care of their grandchild for their irresponsible daughter. On and on it went.

Gaby talked to them all, and she was really getting good at it. It had become a kind of game, separating the fact from the fiction. She got to the point where she could pretty much tell if the person on the other end of that toll-free telephone was telling the truth or not.

Several birth mothers went so far as to fill out the preliminary paperwork consisting of health-screening forms and family profiles. However, it seemed the more we knew, the more problems were revealed and the less desirable the birth mom became. Still, we put in the time. As Stacy and Holly had emphasized from their experience, you never knew for sure which one would be the one.

Gaby talked to a few birth moms off and on for a month or two. We sent money for one to purchase a cellphone so she wouldn't have to call us from the corner pay phone. For one we paid for her rehab clinical visits, for another her maternity clothes. But they all had a way of disappearing.

Then the process would repeat itself—another round of ads, more phone calls, and more uncertainties. Sometimes we'd get three or more calls just in a day. A second round of ads cost another $8,000 and then a third cost $9,000. It was still more of the same: nibbles and bites leading nowhere.

We were on the Cyclone roller coaster like the one I rode as a kid at Lakeside Park near Denver. The first hill was the steepest, the hardest to climb, and the scariest. Then as we went on, it became less scary. It was not the world's fastest roller coaster, but it certainly seemed like the world's longest.

"It's not unusual," Holly told us over the phone. "It can take a while."

"What's a while?" I asked, but I wished I hadn't when I heard her answer.

"For one couple, it took four years, and they weren't even that picky."

At the beginning, I was all right with that time frame. I even welcomed it! The more time it took, I reasoned, the more time I had to adjust to the idea. But the whole process was so draining. We couldn't keep doing this for four years.

We heard stories through the adoption grapevine, a kind of rogues' gallery of adoptions gone wrong. There were tales of adopted children with unexpected, severe emotional or physical problems that turned the adoptive parents' lives into constant struggle.

And then we heard about the big one, the horror of all horrors: the forced return of a child. This happened when the birth mother asked for the child back within the time allotted for her to change her mind. In the adoption game, that seemed to be the worst thing that could happen. If just the loss of the *promise* of a child affected us so deeply, we could not imagine what it would be like to lose a child we had actually held in our arms.

"I knew this single mom," Stacy told us at one of our meetings, "who lived in New Jersey. She was present at the birth of the child she thought would be hers, but after a few days the mother wanted her baby back. The adoptive mom went through that with *five* different birth moms. Yes, five times!"

"Oh, my God!" Gaby said. "How can that be? How can that happen?"

"She wanted a baby so badly she wouldn't give up," Stacy continued. "But she finally succeeded on the sixth attempt. No matter what she lost, no matter what she was going through, she wouldn't stop. She knew there was a baby somewhere out there for her."

"And you're telling us this story to make us feel *good*?" I asked.

Stacy smiled. Gaby and I knew the point Stacy was driving home—that the difference between becoming adoptive parents or not was persistence.

We thought none of the bad things we heard about would happen to us. We thought we were too good at all this. Good at seeing the signs, looking at the forms, reading the doctors' reports, and interpreting information we got from the birth mothers. We thought we were scientific, as if we had the formula to pick a birth mother who would deliver, who would give us a child.

Bullshit!

We fooled ourselves into thinking we could. It was all a crapshoot, a total gamble, and we were losing.

Amber

BEFORE WE KNEW IT, A YEAR AND A HALF had passed since our first meeting with Stacy. Between the ads, the lawyer's fees, the facilitator's fees, and all the other expenses, we had spent about $60,000. I never complained. The process wasn't for the financially fainthearted. Sure, there were ways you could cut corners, streamline the middlemen, but even then it was still expensive. You'd think that after spending that much you would get something. But in those nineteen months we had not gotten even close to meeting one birth mom. Something always happened, and they just had a way of vanishing. We were getting used to being disappointed; we even joked about it.

"Ann has five kids," Gaby said after getting off the phone with another BM. "Two of them live with one ex, the other three with another ex. She wants this one for herself, but her present boyfriend already has three kids and doesn't want another, especially since Ann is still in rehab."

"That would make a great reality show," I said. "The Brady Brunch goes to rehab."

In the beginning we were very diligent, treating each call as if it was our last, even if we felt there was little or no chance that anything would happen. We got to the point where we barely screened them in the beginning and then later narrowed it down to the birth mothers with the most potential.

We were like generals planning for some bizarre battle. We even made a chart for our military campaign. The prospective birth moms were placed on a corkboard with different-colored pins, and we moved them forward or backward depending on how close they were to Babyville. It was all fucking nuts.

At one point, we were communicating with five potential birth mothers. And when I say "we," I mean that I was listening to Gaby doing the communicating. It was a "we" process, but Gaby did the bulk of the work.

Gaby understood that the birth mom needed to trust the adoptive mom—hell, the BM needed to identify with her. Gaby knew that no matter how messed up their lives had been, they needed to be treated with respect and dignity. And no matter how inconsistent their maternal behaviors seemed to be, they were still moms who mostly wanted to do what was right for their child. Many were very specific: "To give my baby all the opportunities I never had."

Gaby was sympathetic toward them. They were looking for a little shelter from all the shit that was going on in their lives, perhaps even a chance at a better life. But if an out-of-work dude on a motorcycle insisted he wanted to raise the baby as his own, the BM would gladly hop on that motorcycle and forget about us.

We heard about the exceptions, though: the BMs at the top, the ones who hadn't been marginalized by poverty, addiction, or both. They had a lifestyle that in many ways was no different from our own. They were the best of all possibilities and the rarest of all the birth moms—the ones from a good home. They were the wholesome teenagers who studied and got good grades, the ones who didn't abuse drugs or alcohol, but just had the misfortune of an unplanned pregnancy. These were the BMs that most adoptive parents dreamed of.

We had just gotten our second round of approval from New York State. The initial license to adopt had expired, so Stacy had to submit an updated application for us. The renewal process was much more streamlined than the initial application and didn't take nearly as long. Around this time, Gaby got a call from Holly telling her about Amber.

"She sounds very sincere," Holly said over speakerphone. That was what she usually said. Her job required her to be heavy on the optimism.

Holly had already gotten us Amber's medical records. We had reached the point where we wouldn't even think of talking to the BM unless we got some information from her first, like medical records and an initial screening form. Inconsistencies were usually a given, so we tried to learn as many details as possible to see if there were any obvious red flags.

Amber seemed to have very few.

She had read our classified ad in the penny saver in Harris County, Texas. She was a thirty-one-year-old mother of two. Her ex-husband had custody of both her kids while she was getting her life back together. She was living with an aunt and uncle near Houston. She was in no position to raise another child.

"I'm not sure why, but I think I have a connection with her," Gaby said after her break-the-ice conversation with Amber. "It was like I was talking to a friend. She's smart and articulate."

"Sounds great. When is she due?" I asked.

"Four months, and it's a girl!" Gaby was excited.

"Great! She sounds like a winner," I said.

But I wasn't too thrilled about her medical screening. In the past she had been a frequent user of marijuana and alcohol. She claimed that she had been free of all drugs and alcohol since she learned she was pregnant. However, had she learned of her pregnancy the day she missed her period or two months later? It made a difference. How long was the baby exposed to all that crap? Regardless, Amber was the most promising birth mother to date.

Gaby got more and more excited as she learned more about Amber. She had done a brief stint in a community college. Sure, there were the bad marriage, bad boyfriends, and many bad choices, but Amber was a good person looking to improve her life and willing to do what was in the best interest of her child.

Two more months passed and it was still a go. Things were looking good. In fact, they were looking so good that we were finally asked to do something we had never yet done: Amber wanted to meet us. To say Gaby was elated would be an understatement. She was thunderstruck.

It was a few weeks before Thanksgiving, and by sheer coincidence we were going to visit my sister and her family in Austin. Houston wasn't that far away. It was all so perfect. Everything was falling into place. It was like finding a parking spot right in front of the restaurant where you had a dinner reservation, on the busiest street in New York City on a Saturday night. And for a New Yorker, believe me, that is a huge deal.

As we waited in our rental car in the parking lot of a strip mall next to an Applebee's restaurant, it was hard for me to fathom where the process had taken us.

This is so frigging crazy.

"You think that's them?" I asked Gaby when a late-model pickup truck drove into the parking lot. Like yellow cabs in New York City, pickup trucks were everywhere in Texas.

"No," Gaby said. There was only a bearded man in the truck.

"Maybe he's a scout, checking us out before they arrive," I speculated.

"Like we're not spying?" Gaby asked.

"I'm not spying. I'd just rather wait here than inside."

"Right," Gaby said. "I think you're more nervous than I am," she added. "Just relax. They're not due for another five minutes."

I couldn't relax. Gaby had established rapport with Amber, enough to feel good about her and the chances of our becoming the parents of her unborn child. I had talked to her only once when I picked up the 888-number phone, and then only because Gaby was in the bathroom.

As we hung out in that parking lot waiting for Amber, I felt like I was waiting for a job interview. An interview for the most important job I'd ever have—one that would last the rest of my life.

"I bet she's fat," I said. "Look at the restaurant she chose, Applebee's. Everything has trans fat in it. I bet they even have a dish called Trans Fat. Besides, Amber is a fat name. I know two Ambers and they're both fat. The dad's probably fat, too. We're going to have a big fat child from Texas. Who's gonna want to hang out with her?"

"Just relax, okay?" Gaby said.

I was rambling. Gaby was only half listening, more focused on the cars driving in. We both felt more comfortable waiting in the car than in the restaurant. Besides, it was easier to escape when you were in your car. Maybe a part of Gaby felt that way, too. What if Amber was right out of a Stephen King novel: overalls, gapped teeth, and carrying a pitchfork? Then what?

I looked at myself in the mirror. My hair was jet black because I'd dyed it the night before.

The constant worry that my age would be a factor in adopting wouldn't go away. Why would any birth mother want a fifty-eight-year-old man to be the adoptive father to her child? It was competitive out there. They had so many choices. Why someone older? I shouldn't even be here. I put my hands on the side of my face and pulled my skin back, tightening it, smoothing out the wrinkles. I looked like I had a botched facelift, like the old Bruce Jenner but with vampire hair. I pulled my skin back even more.

"You sure it doesn't look too dark?" I asked Gaby. "I don't look ridiculous?"

"What?" Gaby answered as if she was not listening.

"My hair, it's not too dark?"

"No, it's fine." She answered too quickly; I knew she was lying. I should have picked a lighter shade like light brown or regular brown, rather than black-black, the color of a vampire's hair.

"Would she notice if I talked to her like this?" I asked Gaby, my voice and face alarmingly distorted from the tightness of the pulled-back skin around my mouth. I looked like I was inside a wind tunnel for testing jet planes where a 200-miles-an-hour wind flattened my face.

Gaby barely looked at me.

"I should have gotten Botox," I went on. "Why didn't you let me get Botox?"

Gaby shook her head. "You're being an idiot. You look great for your age. You look at least ten years younger than you are."

"Only ten years?" I was alarmed. That was still old. Who adopts a kid at forty-eight, let alone fifty-eight? I was going for thirty-eight!

"You know dentists are doing Botox now? I could have done it myself. Or I could try Scotch tape to pull my skin back," I said, trying to pass the time by brainstorming. "You know the really clear kind? I still have time—there's a CVS right over there," I said, pointing.

Gaby shook her head again and partially closed her eyes to appear even more dismissive to my ridiculous suggestions.

The longer we waited, the more nervous I became.

Car after car, and truck after truck pulled into the parking lot, each one a false alarm. And then this shiny green Ford SuperCrew, the mother of all four-wheel-drive trucks, drove into the lot. Three passengers were inside—a man and two women. I knew this was the one. Somehow, we both knew. We didn't say anything; we just stared at the truck as if we were watching an alien ship landing.

Without a word, Gaby got out of the car and walked straight over. I didn't move. I held back and watched. A woman about my age got out of the truck, perhaps the aunt. She was followed by a gray-haired man—the uncle, maybe? Next had to be Amber. I held my breath.

She was about five-foot-three or -four, medium build, light color skin—the same skin and hair color as Gaby. In fact, she looked like she could pass for Gaby's pregnant sister. Could this really be the one we were searching for? What were the chances, the odds of finding a birth mom who resembled my wife? Fate was involved; it had to be. This was the hand of God. Good things came to those who were patient, right? I watched Gaby hug Amber, and for a moment the divineness of it all overwhelmed me. I finally got out of the car to meet them.

"Hi, Amber," I said, looking into her eyes, trying to get a read. I held out my hand. She took it, and then she hugged me.

"So glad you made it, Michael," Amber said.

"Vernon Fletcher," the man said with a firm grip and a deep Texas accent. "Pleasure."

"Agnes Fletcher," the woman I'd pegged as the aunt said as she hugged me and kissed me on the cheek. "Michael is such a nice name," she said with a sweet, silky Southern drawl.

Hugs were everywhere as if this were a family reunion. We made our way toward the restaurant.

Sitting in the back of the Applebee's, I started to relax. I listened but I couldn't take my eyes off Amber. I studied her. She seemed so normal. Gaby and Amber did most of the talking as if they were old friends who hadn't seen each other in a long time.

I was, and still am, so amazed by Gaby's perseverance, by her dogged determination to do whatever was necessary to finish the adoption process. And I was blown away even more by the warmth and compassion she gave to Amber. It was a blessing to have a wife whose depth and inner beauty kept on giving and giving. I was so proud of her.

"How are you feeling, Amber?" Gaby asked.

"Great. And I want to thank you again for the maternity clothes. It was so nice of you."

"It was our pleasure to do that for you," Gaby said. "And if there is anything else you need, just let us know."

They chatted while I sat like a dumb ass.

"It's hot here," I said to Vernon.

He nodded.

"And the traffic's not bad," I added. The conversation sounded a bit forced and sporadic, like tuning a radio, looking for the best reception.

"Well, I'm sure New York gets a whole lot more traffic," Vernon said. "Things are plenty busy enough for me around here."

I nodded in agreement. "It's nice around here."

"Never been to New York," Aunt Agnes chimed in. "Always wanted to go, though."

And then I heard Amber say something that shocked me nearly out of my shoes. "What are you going to name her?"

Fuck me, did she really ask that? This is really happening. Names? Who even thinks of naming a child that's not yours . . . not yet?

Gaby was so smart. I didn't know she had already thought of names. She was prepared for everything, like someone who did the homework before the teacher assigned it.

Gaby rattled off three names. "We like Chloe, Abigail, and Samantha."

We do? This was the first I'd heard about it. Amber too looked surprised, like a prosecutor who was taken aback when the defendant answered the question that blew away the case. Was she testing us?

Gaby continued to take charge of the conversation. "How about you, Amber? What names do you like?"

"I like Elphaba, after my grandmother," she answered.

"Beautiful name," Aunt Agnes agreed.

"Elphaba, that's a great name," Gaby replied.

I don't know how Gaby kept a straight face.

Are you fucking kidding me? Elphaba? I wanted to vomit. This girl was going to be bat mitzvahed, not playing the lead in *Wicked.*

"I like that name, don't you, honey?" Gaby looked directly at me without even the hint of a smirk.

Shit. I swallowed. My mouth was dry. *We like Ruth, Rachel, or Sarah. You know, good old biblical Jewish names.*

Instead, I said, "Yes, I do. That's unique." *If you lived in fucking Salem.*

I was so glad the topic of religion didn't come up. But we had the bases covered. "Gaby grew up Catholic," was all that we would say, hoping they wouldn't ask me. If they did ask me, would I say, "I know I look it, but I'm not Jewish," if it meant getting a kid? Then I'd probably feel guilty for all the sacrifices Jews had suffered in the past in the name of religious freedom. Had distant relatives of Vernon, Agnes, and Amber ever lynched someone down here because they were Jewish? We knew that some people still considered Jews undesirable. So, although we had decided to raise our child Jewish, we had the Christian trump card ready.

Lunch lasted over an hour. I liked Amber. I liked Agnes. I bonded with Vernon, who was a nice guy and a car fanatic. I loved cars, too. Growing up in Colorado in the sixties, I thought cars were everything.

"You should come to the New York International Auto Show sometime. It's one of the biggest in the country," I told him.

"I'd like that very much," Vernon replied.

I wanted to be friendly, but I knew that no matter how this all worked out, I'd probably never see Vernon or Agnes again.

Back in the parking lot, we hugged and kissed goodbye. A simple strong handshake was goodbye enough for Vernon and me. Gaby and I waited and watched as Amber, Vernon, and Agnes got into their SuperCrew, then waved to them like a couple saying goodbye to long-lost relatives as they drove away.

It couldn't have gone better. For the first time, I was encouraged—convinced, even—that we were soon going to be parents. Gaby had tears in her eyes and I did, too. We held each other's hand with the tight squeeze of promise.

For the next month, through Stacy, we happily sent Amber money for more maternity clothes, tuition for a course at a beauty school, and money to maintain her cellphone. Whatever she needed, within reason, we sent. We wanted to make her comfortable. After all, she was the birth mother of our child-to-be. We wanted to ease any tension in her life so that her pregnancy would be as stress-free as possible. If Amber was taken care of and had less to worry about, that had to be good for the baby.

Gaby insisted that we buy a crib and some baby clothes for our girl. I thought it was too soon. But Gaby, in her mind, had already become a mom. She prepared as if it was inevitable. Our second bedroom officially became the nursery.

It was a great, upbeat month. One month until delivery. Things couldn't be going more smoothly.

Then one day Amber didn't return Gaby's phone call.

"She always calls back the same day," Gaby said with a worried look on her face. "Maybe something happened."

"Give her until tomorrow and then try again. I wouldn't make a big deal of it."

Gaby called the next day and left a message. Still, Amber did not return her phone call. Gaby called the next day and the next. No response. She was in a state of panic.

"What's happened to her? Maybe she had an accident or got sick. I'm really worried."

"Maybe something came up," I answered. "She has two other kids to worry about." But it didn't look good.

Both Stacy and Holly tried to get in touch with Amber. We wrote letters. We left messages.

"Still no luck," Gaby said, having just gotten off the phone with Holly.

"We were warned that this could happen," I said. "It's happened before. Sometimes they just disappear, back to wherever they felt comfortable."

"But not Amber," Gaby countered. "We had a connection. She asked us what we going to name her, our daughter. *Our daughter!*"

Two weeks later Amber's phone didn't ring at all, and we discovered that it had been disconnected. We were at the end of a dark rope. Desperate for answers, we called her aunt Agnes and uncle Vernon. I made the call. Gaby was too nervous to do it. She didn't want to face the obvious truth. Vernon answered, and he was friendly and nice but to the point.

"I never trusted that girl," he admitted. "Even though she's my niece on my wife's side, I still never trusted her. We paid for everything, and then she meets this tattoo artist, Jake, and a few days later, he asks her to move in with him. He tells her he wants to be the father of her baby. So she up and leaves and takes off to live with him someplace north of here. I'm sorry. You folks were so nice."

Vernon talked in more detail, but I barely listened. The rest didn't matter. I felt that his compassion was sincere.

"Well, I guess she fooled us all," I said. "And thank you for telling us." There wasn't much else left to say.

"You're welcome," Vernon said. "And take care."

"Goodbye," I said, and hung up the phone.

Gaby knew the news wasn't good.

"I don't get it. How could she do that?" Gaby asked. "What the *fook*! It doesn't make sense."

"None of it makes sense," I agreed.

"What's wrong with her? How could she do this to us?" Gaby asked.

"We're not dealing with normal people," I said.

It confirmed all my prejudices, my suspicions about what happens when you deal with people who set their standards and values lower than yours.

"A fucking lowlife," I concluded to Gaby.

Sure, it was a derogatory thing to say, but it summed up how I felt. Was I being fair? Amber came from a different place than we did. She'd been a victim her whole life, and that was all she knew: life was a dog-eat-dog world. Did she even think about the pain she was causing others? Would I have done the same under similar circumstances, I wondered? I hoped not. I hoped that no matter how bad life got, I'd still be able to respect others and their feelings, to be honest, and to do the honorable thing. But she was abused, abandoned, marginalized. That was still no excuse. She shouldn't have treated us that way.

She's a lowlife, a wacko. I don't give a shit if I'm not being fair.

"Was it something I said?" Gaby continued to try to figure it out. She couldn't let it go. "What went wrong? We gave her whatever she wanted."

We looked inward for answers, for a rational reason why it had happened. There was no real answer; it was beyond our control. Still, we felt guilty that we hadn't done something more.

"It had nothing to do with what we did," I said. "Any couple could have played the part, but the outcome would have been the same. We did everything right. It was a control thing. It gave her power. She just didn't care enough to be open and honest. Amber wasn't who we thought she was."

"*Fook, fook, fook,*" Gaby said, looking numb and exhausted.

It was the only word that did justice to how Gaby felt—the only word that seemed to grab the depth of her exasperation.

I joined her. It was almost a chant for us. "Fuck, *fook,* fuck, *fook.*" The melodious sound of it, the absurdity of such a base word made musical, somehow lessened our pain, and for a moment we smiled, then laughed, lost in the ridiculousness of it all.

"Fuck! *Fook!* Fuck! *Fook!*"

We then sat quietly for a moment.

"What are we going to do now?" Gaby asked. "Can you still do this?"

"I don't know," I answered, but I knew she was asking for herself. "Can you?" I asked.

Gaby wasn't built to give up. Why would anyone want to go through all this again and again? And for how long? How long could we let these nut jobs be a part of our lives? We were playing their game, by their rules. And in the end what had we gotten? Nothing. We were back where we started. Our emotional roller coaster had crashed at the bottom of a steep hill and wasn't going anywhere. Should we repair it, put it back on track, restart the engine, and head back up the hill? Or should we just get off here? Was it the end of the line for us?

One way or another, we had to let go of all the hurt and bitterness in order to move on.

If at first you don't succeed, try, try again. Isn't that what they say? Isn't that what people who are successful practice, persistence? You get up, dust off your pants, and move on. But how deep does the loss have to be before you stop? At what price is it no longer worth it?

People experience loss all the time, and they die a thousand deaths over the course of a lifetime from losses they have suffered. Most have no choice. But we did. We could have stopped the hurt right then. No one would have blamed us for stopping. We had nothing but an empty crib and unworn baby clothes in a vacant room waiting for a child. We could remove those reminders. We could return to our other life, the one before adoption. We could go to Bali. But neither of us wanted that.

We were a strong, loving couple, made even stronger by the ordeal we had just gone through. How long had we been trying? Could it be nearly five years since the decision to have a child really started us on this journey?

We had come so far. It wasn't the time to give up. We were willing to do whatever it took to get there. Besides, Bali was just a place we wanted to visit; adoption was a place where we wanted to live. The idea of a child was now in our bones, our reality.

If we had quit, I knew the relief wouldn't have lasted. I knew Gaby.

She would have had regrets. I would have had regrets. This wasn't over by any means. We were wounded, but not dead. Other people picked up and moved on. That was what we needed to do. We couldn't quit.

I took her hand. She squeezed my hand right back. I knew what she needed to hear.

"Honey, who in their right mind would want to name their child Elphaba?"

Gaby smiled. "I know. I was thinking that, too. It's the worst, isn't it?"

"You know, I don't think she was even really pregnant. I think it was just a pillow under there. She just wanted a free meal at Applebee's."

Gaby laughed. "And the colors she wore. Who wears pink with orange? It was disgusting."

"Disgusting" said with a French accent made it sound even worse.

"We just have to make sure that Holly doesn't advertise in that paper for the next round," I said.

"That's for sure." Gaby smiled more, and I knew that she had enough strength for another round. We called Holly.

PART V

PRIZEFIGHT

CHAPTER 21

Ashley

THE NEXT SEVEN MONTHS PASSED BY very quickly. We paid for five more rounds of ads. It was built into our monthly budget. We were heading upriver with our engines running at full steam. The shoreline was familiar, lined with dozens and dozens of the usual screenings, glimmers of hope, and false starts. Sometimes we were the ones who hopped off the boat, deciding the birth moms had taken too many drugs, drunk too much alcohol, or had too much negative medical history.

But often the BMs were the ones jumping ship. First they were wildly enthusiastic. *I can't wait to meet you both. You guys would be the perfect parents for my baby.* Then there would be lies and excuses, until one day they had gone or decided to keep the child.

And so, after nearly $30,000 worth of more ads and legal fees, we still had come up empty.

"How much have you spent in all?" Richard had asked, knowing how expensive the process was.

"I'm not sure," I answered. "Maybe around $100,000."

"No fucking way. Shit!" Richard said. "I should have sold you one of my kids."

We were discouraged, but not devastated. All that stress and tension could have been the end for other couples, but somehow it made us even stronger and closer. We had become accustomed to the disappointments. It was a way of life.

"I forgot to tell you," Gaby told me one morning over breakfast. "You're not going to believe what Mary Beth told me last night."

"Who?" I asked.

"She's the ICBM from New Mexico."

Some birth mothers we called ICBMs, for intercontinental ballistic birth mothers. They were like a missile that had gone astray, one that could explode at any moment.

"I thought she was out of the picture," I said.

"We all did, but she called me back," Gaby enlightened me.

"What did she say?"

"It's crazy," Gaby continued. "She said the reason she didn't call us back was . . ." Gaby just stopped and shook her head before she continued.

"What?" I asked.

"You're going to appreciate this. She said she went to see her gynecologist. But she was so high, she ended up at the dentist's office next door. The dentist asked her what the problem was, and she told him she had pain when she urinated."

"Maybe she was brushing too hard," I joked.

Gaby laughed. "That's a good one. But she wanted painkillers. The dentist called the police and she was arrested."

I shook my head in disbelief.

The birth mothers' crazy, marginalized, living-on-the-edge existence became ours. I became less hostile. I began to understand who they were. They reacted on the fly, moving from one obstacle to the next, taking one step forward and then two steps back. Their circumstances were often so abysmal that I wondered how anyone could ever escape the trap that life had caught them in.

We gave as much of ourselves as we could, hoping in the end it would pay off. We became more flexible in our qualifications. We went from seeking a newborn to a baby under two years old, from a birth mom who wasn't a drug user to one who only occasionally used drugs, alcohol, or tobacco. We opened our options to almost any birth mom who would give us the chance to be parents. Beggars can't be choosers, and all that sort of thing.

It was a Monday morning when Gaby got the call from Holly telling her about another birth mom, Ashley. It sounded promising. She lived in Shreveport, Louisiana. She was twenty-nine years old and had a seven-year-old son, Beau. It was a complicated story.

Ashley was living with her husband, Art, in a sexless marriage of convenience. She'd been an unemployed single mom when she met him. He was an older man who wanted a family, and Ashley offered a package deal: herself and her son, for a home and a man with a job.

Of course, as you would expect, their marriage deteriorated until they were more like roommates than husband and wife. It sounded like an open marriage. That would explain why Ashley had started seeing an ex-boyfriend.

Big surprise, Ashley got pregnant. Art threatened to kick her out if she kept the child. He wasn't about to take care of another baby. And the ex-boyfriend was living with his parents, so taking on a family wasn't in the cards. Ashley was against having an abortion.

Still, she was hopeful that somehow things would change. She fantasized that her ex-boyfriend would eventually get a better job and move out of his parents' house so they could get a place together. Or if that didn't work, she hoped her husband would have a change of heart and let her stay with the new baby. Neither of those plans had worked out. Ashley had run out of options. She was eight months pregnant when she saw our ad, and out of desperation she contacted Holly.

Gaby called Ashley right after she spoke to Holly. As I listened, it sounded typical from my end, although there was none of that uncomfortable rambling I had been accustomed to hearing as Gaby tried to connect with a birth mom. It sounded simple, like two people just trying to get to know each other. "Where are you from originally? How many brothers and sisters do you have? What's your son's favorite subject in school?" All that normal stuff. And also, "And you're expecting a girl? Fantastic!"

Most birth moms were considering other adoptive parents, even if they said otherwise. There was no way of knowing how many. According to Holly there were usually at least one or two other couples in the mix. In this case, Holly found out, Ashley was talking to only one other couple. We didn't ask anything about them because we didn't really want to know. We wanted this to be about us, not the competition. Gaby's French accent had to be a plus. It was so exotic, and also the Cajuns down in Louisiana spoke a form of French. It had to give us an edge over other couples. Or maybe it didn't. Wasn't the Klan down there? And didn't they hate just about everyone, foreigners and Jews included?

Twenty minutes later, the conversation was over. It sounded to me like a smooth, tight comedy set: laughter in all the right spots, not too long or too short—just right.

"It feels different this time," Gaby explained. "I know I've said that before, but something's really different—she seems so sincere. She's bright and warm. I really like her."

"That's great," I replied.

Sure, Gaby had great insight when it came to others and could easily see through the phoniness more than I could. But Amber had fooled her—fooled us both. Gaby had to be guarded. What's that saying: fool me once, shame on you; fool me twice, shame on me? Anyway, I couldn't imagine it would happen again to us. *Lightning can't strike you down twice, right? What were the chances?*

"This is the one, honey," Gaby said. "I'm not sure why, but somehow I know it. I feel it in my bones." Gaby was convinced Ashley was it—our birth mom. She convinced me, too.

A few days later we got another call from Holly. Apparently Ashley liked our adoption album and had made a decision. "Good news. You're it!" Holly said. "You're the only couple in the running."

"Oh, my God, I can't believe it," Gaby said into the speakerphone. "I had a feeling that Ashley was the one."

It was now a race to the finish line and the winner was a given—us. Gaby's premonition was coming true.

From there it all happened so quickly. More comprehensive medical reports and histories were filled out and returned in days. Gaby spoke to Ashley at least once daily, sometimes twice. We were taking no prisoners; our only mission was to get that baby. And the scout who was leading us there was none other than the birth mother herself, Ashley. Three weeks never passed so quickly. I'd forgotten that Ashley was due very soon.

On June 14, Gaby got a phone call from Holly. We knew that Ashley was slightly overdue. The doctor had decided that if Ashley didn't start labor soon, she would induce it as early as Tuesday—in two days. We should come to Louisiana as soon as possible. Stacy was racing through the paperwork. It was full speed ahead. Gaby called me at my office: one Sunday a month I saw patients.

"Now? I can't believe it!" I said. A patient was behind me in the treatment chair, the dental assistant seated next to her. The patient's mom was standing nearby. Everyone looked at me, not certain if it was happiness, anger, good news, or bad news. I was smiling when I got off the phone. My office manager, Rachel, rushed over when she heard me shout.

"Cancel my patients for the rest of the week," I said. "We're going to Louisiana to get a baby!"

"Oh, my God!" Rachel said.

My mind exploded in anticipation as I called the airline for reservations. Gaby was standing next to me. I could have tapped the number in the dark; Gaby's ear-to-ear smile would have lit up the darkest of rooms. She was on her way to catch her dream; her desire to be a mom was now close to becoming a reality. She could taste it. Her joy was contagious.

We booked the first flight out the next day. In fifteen hours, we would be on our way. Neither of us could sleep that night. Spooning in a face-on embrace, we grinned at each other the entire night.

We headed to the airport on Monday morning at 5:45 without any obstacles or dreaded phone calls to stop us. There were no direct flights, so we had a two-hour layover in Houston and then a connection that arrived in Shreveport at 4:30 p.m. Everything was happening so fast. It had become surreal for us both.

Once on the ground, we looked up and down the list of Hertz preferred customers posted on the electronic bulletin board.

"We're 143," Gaby said as she found our name. As we walked toward our car, I turned my cellphone off airplane mode. There was a missed call from Stacy.

No, I thought, suddenly feeling a pang of dread. *Not now.*

At this stage a call couldn't be a good thing. I was anxious as I listened to the message.

"Stacy says not to worry, but we should call her as soon as we land," I said as I repeated the message to Gaby. Whenever someone says not to worry, the first thing you're going to do is *fucking* worry.

Gaby looked distressed. "You'd better call and see what it is."

I was the one who returned such calls. Somehow that had become my job: the screener of bad tidings, the filter who took the bad news and somehow made it sound not quite as awful. It rarely worked, but that was the idea. Gaby had so much invested emotionally. She was closer to the BMs than I was, hearing their stories firsthand; sharing their views on motherhood, children, and life; bonding as only another woman could. Macho or not, I wanted to be protective, to be the buffer. I wanted to shield her as much as I could from a direct hit—one that went right to the heart.

"Not great news, but not terrible," Stacy started out. I tried to maintain my fake smile as Gaby watched and listened. I'm sure she saw right through my act, though, because I probably looked more nauseous than happy.

"The biological dad still hasn't signed the papers," I repeated to Gaby a split second after hearing it from Stacy. Both parents had to sign off on the papers in order to release the child legally into someone else's custody. Parental rights had to be protected.

"Well, what does that mean?" I asked. "When is he going to sign?" *Does that mean we should return to New York, wait, or what?*

"We're working on it, "Stacy continued. "We usually like everything signed before the delivery. But sometimes things happen so quickly that we don't have time. The attorney we're working with down there is talking to the birth dad. Apparently, he is a little confused. Ashley is with him now, trying to persuade him to sign the documents."

"Okay, that's good," I said.

"It shouldn't be a problem," Stacy said. "I just wanted to give you a heads-up. Check in to your hotel, and I'll call you as soon as I know more."

"Okay, I appreciate that," I said. "And thanks for letting us know." I knew what she was doing: softening the blow if it came, if we had to turn around and go home because of the dad. This time it was the dad. The birth-fucking-father—a real *BFF*!

I put the phone in my pocket. "So, it's not terrible," I said. "The birth father hasn't signed yet, but the attorney is talking with him. No big deal. He just has some questions before he signs."

Gaby was annoyed. "Terry? What questions? What's wrong with him? What questions?" He had a name, Terry. *BFF Terry.*

"Stacy said it's not uncommon, especially when things move so fast. It's just a small glitch. Let's go check in to the hotel. We have a meeting with Ashley at six thirty p.m. Stacy will call us. I'm sure he'll sign."

Gaby didn't look so sure as she withdrew into silence. If Terry had been there, he would have heard a thing or two from Gaby. But he wasn't, so all we could do was wait.

We were just there to get our baby and go.

Our baby! That was the first time I had even thought in those terms. *Our baby* was so close, and it was up to all the others to make it happen. We were again caught in a current and unable to swim ashore. We needed the birth parents. They were the only ones who could get us out, who could throw us the rope and help us to land. They didn't need us. We needed them more than they could imagine.

Our hotel was about a half hour from the airport, and it was a quiet, somber drive. Originally we'd asked for a suite with a kitchen, but it was booked and we were on a waiting list. None of that seemed important now. Everything was on hold.

We both sat on the edge of the king-size bed. Two overloaded extended-stay suitcases lay on the floor in front of us.

"Well, I guess I should start unpacking," Gaby said, looking for motivation.

"I guess so," I said. I got up and began to place one of the suitcases on the bed when the 888-number phone rang.

"I'll get it," I said as I went for the phone that stuck out of the side pocket of Gaby's purse.

Gaby got to it first and looked at the caller ID. "It's Ashley," she said as she answered the call.

"Yes, we're here," Gaby said. "Oh, okay. I was going to ask you about that. Great. Really? That's so great. Okay. Looking forward to it. We'll see you soon." Gaby put the phone down. "He signed!" she exclaimed.

It always amazes me how the right words can make all the anxiety and pain go away. Like "I love you" from the girl you have a crush on, or "The test was negative" from a nurse on the phone—or in this case, "He signed."

"Yes!" I said. Signaling our sudden change in mood, we high-fived each other. We continued unpacking in a day that was much brighter than it had been a few seconds ago.

We arrived at the restaurant a little before 6:30 p.m. We were early. The place was packed with the early dinner crowd. In New York City, 6:30 p.m. was the time when elderly people or people who didn't have the connections to get a prime-time reservation came to eat. No one seemed to be waiting for us—at least not anyone who was very pregnant. We sat on chairs near the hostess desk and waited.

"I'll be right back," I said to Gaby.

"You going to the bathroom again? You just went at the hotel."

"So?" I said. "Are you rationing my bathroom visits?"

"I know you. You're going to check yourself out in the mirror again."

"Or maybe I'm just nervous and I have to pee," I said.

"I'm sorry—you're right. Just hurry in case she gets here."

I walked toward the bathroom. Gaby was right. I was going to check myself out in the bathroom mirror. I had a lipstick-size tube of foundation that I had recently bought to smooth out my skin and give me that "youthful glow." At least that was what the advertisement said. I applied it to my cheeks, straightened out my hair, then took a portable toothbrush from my pocket and quickly brushed my teeth. I was prepared. I looked at my smile in the mirror again. My teeth were clean. I studied myself for a moment. *Think young. You're cool. That's right . . . you got it!* I pulled my skin back and stared at the mirror until I was satisfied that I looked younger. I closed my eyes to seal in the younger attitude, and then I was off.

Gaby was where I had left her.

"You look beautiful," she said.

"Thank you," I replied. "It's my youthful glow."

Gaby smiled and shook her head as if to say, *Yeah, right.* I wasn't fooling anyone. I looked at my watch. It was 6:42, fashionably late.

Looking outside through the glass door, I saw a young woman get out of her car near the front of the restaurant. She had brown hair and wore skinny jeans. She wasn't conspicuously pregnant. It wasn't her.

"Not yet," I said as I sat back down next to Gaby.

The brown-haired woman walked into the restaurant. She looked right at me.

"You're Michael," she said warmly. Ashley had our pictures from the adoption album. There was no photo requirement for the BM. Although some people requested one, we never did.

"Ashley?" I said.

"Yes, it's me," she answered.

I got up and hugged her. "I'm so happy to finally meet you," I said. *What's with the belly?* I wanted to ask. *You have no belly.*

I was okay with just a handshake. But the stakes were high, and I had to step up my game. I knew a kiss or a hug to move things along would make Gaby happy.

I need to see a belly. You have no pregnant belly.

Gaby was standing next to me and anxious to do her part. "Ashley!" Gaby cried before hugging and kissing her. "It's you, it's really you!"

Gaby's hugs and kisses lasted a lot longer than mine did, and they were certainly more heartfelt.

I looked more pregnant than Ashley. Beer-bellied male friends of mine looked like they were having triplets compared to her. Gaby and I looked at each other, and I knew she must be thinking the same thing I was: *Where is the fucking belly?*

As we followed the hostess to our table, I couldn't stop thinking about it. Was this a scam? I tried to sneak a better look at Ashley's profile; maybe I'd missed something. She had a little bump, maybe, but that was it. She wasn't wearing maternity clothes, just jeans and a long, untucked denim shirt. And she wasn't waddling like a penguin when she walked, either.

Gaby started the conversation as we took our seats. "It seems like I've known you forever."

"Me, too," Ashley concurred.

They chatted like old friends who hadn't seen each other in a while. I couldn't get my mind off the way Ashley's flat stomach looked. It was too distracting.

I wanted to say, "How many months along are you?" But instead it came out, "How come you don't have a belly?"

"I know, I don't show much, do I? Everyone tells me that, but it's there, believe me."

Ashley lifted her shirt up. And there it was, the big belly. She was definitely pregnant, but when she put the shirt back down her bump nearly disappeared, as if by magic. That would be a great Vegas nightclub magic act. *"Now I'm pregnant, now I'm not."*

"I have to admit, I was a little nervous, too," Gaby said. "You're so thin."

"I was the same with my first. I guess some people just gain less weight."

"Lucky you," Gaby said. "By the way, I'm so glad Terry finally signed the papers."

"He can be a real jerk sometimes. He was worried that I wouldn't see him anymore. What an idiot."

"So, is he okay with everything now?" I chimed in.

"He's on board one hundred percent," Ashley said. "You guys are so cute together," she added, changing the subject matter. "You look just like your pictures," she continued without a hint of sarcasm as she looked right at me.

"Thank you," Gaby replied.

Don't ask how old I am. Please don't ask me how old I am.

Ashley drank iced tea between bites of her hamburger. I wasn't crazy about her having the iced tea, caffeine being a stimulant and all, but better that than cola. Cola not only had caffeine, but didn't it have all that other crap that could dissolve a penny as well? None of that could be good for an unborn baby.

There were moments of silence. We were strangers brought together by one thing: a baby. Even though we all wanted the same thing—a wonderful and loving home for the baby—the results had to be different: for us, joy; for Ashley, sorrow. Even if everything went perfectly and according to plan, there would still be that underlying hurt of giving up a child that was a constant in the dynamic. *So much tension!*

So of course there would be moments of silence and awkwardness, because we all knew what was at stake.

The whole prospective father thing was making me a little nuts, a little neurotic. We didn't even have the child yet, but the notion of her physical proximity, right there in Ashley's belly, made it more real. I wanted to grab the iced tea and take it away from her. *Don't you know that shit's not good for your baby? Give me that!* As a precaution, I sat on my hands and watched her drink.

In Gaby I sensed the pressure even more, the stress of unfinished business. Our adoption experiences had made us gun-shy, and that stuff with Terry, the birth father, clearly showed us how paranoid we had become—how fearful of being exposed to more pain. We were walking deeper into the woods without a map, and we were scared. We knew where we wanted to go; we just weren't sure if we were ever going to get there. So many obstacles were still in our way. So many things could still go wrong. We knew the risks. But we were now so close. If all went well, if we got the baby when she was born, then all we had to do was wait. The waiting period for Louisiana was five days for private adoption, not counting the day of birth. That meant that a day after the baby was born, the birth mother had five days to change her mind, even if she had signed the surrender papers. If she didn't change her mind, we would be out of the forest and into the sunshine in less than a week. Then we could do the happy dance and breathe a big collective sigh of relief. The baby would officially be ours.

"Ah, she's kicking," Ashley said as she touched her belly. "You want to feel her?"

"Sure," Gaby said as she gently put her hand on Ashley's belly.

"Wait," Ashley said. "She usually follows with another one. There she goes."

"I do. I feel her," Gaby said. "You try."

"No thanks," I said. "I'll pass for now." I wasn't quite ready for that. I was afraid—of what, I wasn't quite sure.

"Are you ready for tomorrow?" Ashley asked as we waited for the check.

"Yes, aren't we, honey?" Gaby responded.

I nodded up and down, but inside I wasn't sure if I was ready at all.

Stacy had informed us that they weren't going to wait to induce delivery. In addition to Ashley's labor delay, the position of the baby wasn't ideal. The obstetrician felt that rather than wait another day or two for natural labor, it would be better for the baby and the mother to induce labor tomorrow, a Tuesday.

Like a chant the word rang through my head. *Tomorrow!*

"They said we should be at the hospital by seven a.m.," Ashley told us as we all hugged our good-byes in the parking lot.

"See you in the morning," Gaby said.

That was less than twelve hours away: a long time to endure the kind of anxiety that comes with the delivery of a child.

Gaby was elated. For her, tomorrow couldn't arrive soon enough.

CHAPTER 22

You Have a Girl—or Not

I HAD NO IDEA WHAT A DELIVERY WAS going to be like. I had zero expectations, just notions based on scattered words I had heard here and there—words like "hospital registration," "delivery protocol," "car seat," and more. I wasn't being cavalier, nor was I just along for the ride. Part of me just didn't believe any of it, and that part just stood by, letting the events unfold. Then there was that other part, the part of me that wanted to take charge, make it happen, embrace the circumstances, and whisk that child away. That part of me waited impatiently.

We stood in the lobby of the hospital. We had arrived early, 6:35 a.m. Neither of us had slept very well.

"See, she's on time," Gaby said to me as we watched Ashley approach the glass doors.

I couldn't put my finger on it, but there was something about Ashley that just didn't feel right. She was being cool about the whole thing—maybe too cool.

We hugged Ashley. It was a good start for the big day.

She was accompanied by another woman. "This is my mom, Sharon," Ashley said.

"Nice to meet you," Gaby said as she hugged Sharon. "I have heard so much about you."

That was news to me. Sharon looked like no mom I had ever seen, not among the thousands of other mothers I had met.

Sharon was in her fifties. She had blond hair, almost a buzz cut. The short sleeves of her shirt were tightly rolled up to her shoulders. Her outfit was completed by cut-off jeans and high-top black sneakers with no socks. Sharon's arms and legs were riddled with tattoos. Body piercings were everywhere. And her smell! She reeked of tobacco, like a permanent cloud of the stuff floated above her. Still, I held my breath and went in for the hug, but instead she took my hand and shook it with a strong, almost painful grip. It was one of those macho, I-can-squeeze-harder-than-you grips.

"Nice meeting you," I said, knowing instantly I didn't like her.

Sharon didn't say anything but just half smiled. She had the charm of a Hells Angel and dressed like one, too. From where I stood, there was a lot to dislike.

The four of us immediately went to the registration desk. Holly had faxed the necessary papers to the hospital, and they were ready for us. Since this was a private hospital, Ashley—or in this case, Gaby and I—were required to pay in advance for service. I knew the costs and fees had been discussed at some point, but I had only a vague recollection of them. Sure, we had already spent a small fortune, but wasn't it worth it all, I asked myself? Wasn't this the closest we had been? Still, it felt like we were traveling deeper into an uncharted jungle without any guarantee we'd ever get out.

Gaby wrote the check from our joint account as I watched. It was for nearly $5,000. Ashley got some government assistance and her obstetrician accepted her Medicaid, but the rest was on us, the adoptive parents, or the APs—our official name that we were stuck with at the hospital. I wasn't crazy about that. There had to be another term. Better Parents? No, that would be presumptuous and arrogant. How about "alternative parents?" I liked that one, and you could even keep the same acronym.

Gaby and I waited in the lobby while the nurse wheeled Ashley up to her room to prepare for delivery. Wheelchairs for pregnant women were mandatory once they were admitted. Sharon walked by her side with what had become her constant frown. She was giving off a lot of negative vibes—vibes that said she was not happy with her daughter's decision to give up her unborn grandchild.

"So let me get this straight," I said to Gaby. "She's checking in to her room, and then in about an hour she's scheduled to deliver the actual baby?"

"Honey, why are you such an idiot when it comes to this stuff?"

"I know I am." I knew I was being stupid, but the whole baby-delivery process was a mystery to me. Richard, who had witnessed several births, summed it up for me: "It's like watching a six-pound bowling ball coming out of someone's butt." Even if his description was an exaggeration, it had to be a very painful and difficult process. And yet women did it all the time. They were so much stronger than men could ever hope to be.

I dropped my thoughts of the delivery and switched to something else.

"So, you're not going to say anything about her mom?" I asked.

"No," Gaby said emphatically.

"I know you're trying to stay positive. But that lady is a pill."

"She's a character for sure," Gaby said, trying to sugarcoat it.

"Okay, I can go along with that. And what a talker," I added.

"Michael, enough."

The baby, the baby, I repeated in my mind, trying to get to that happy place, away from the land of skepticism, cynicism, and thoughts of Sharon, the grandmama. I was working hard not to focus on the negativity.

Gaby looked at her watch. "It's been twenty minutes. The nurses should have gotten Ashley ready by now. Let's go."

As far as hospitals went, this place had a lot going for it. It was modern, clean, and seemingly efficient. Room 22 was a private room. Hey, and why not private—it was on us.

Sharon was sitting by the bed when we walked into the busy room. One nurse was taking Ashley's vitals. Another nurse was prepping her. We stood and watched it all.

A short woman in surgical scrubs came into the room. "Hi, I'm Dr. Groda," she said, shaking each of our hands with a big smile on her face. She seemed happy that we were there.

According to Stacy, Dr. Groda was a strong advocate for our adoption. She knew Ashley well, having delivered her as well as her first baby. She felt that Ashley was not capable of raising another child and it would be a big mistake. It wasn't just the lack of money, but the lack of stability in Ashley's life. Although sweet, Ashley was irresponsible and emotionally unstable. She would often leave her young son with her mother or husband and disappear for days. And the husband and grandmama were, big surprise, equally poor caregivers.

Dr. Groda was very forthright. She explained to us that all the delivery rooms in the hospital were currently occupied, so they were going to set up the hospital room for the delivery.

The nurse started an IV of Pitocin to induce labor, and we stood back and watched as a parade of nurses, technicians, and hospital staff brought equipment into the room. It was amazing. In less than fifteen minutes, Room 22 looked like an O.R. It was 8:30 a.m. and everything was in place. We were just waiting for Ashley to be dilated enough to deliver. Sharon left the room; I was sure she went for a smoke.

"How long does it usually take?" I asked Leslie, a maternity nurse who had introduced herself to us earlier. She looked to be in her late thirties: cute, calm, and very sweet.

"She's somewhat dilated, so probably a few hours—sometimes more," Leslie answered. "You guys must be so excited."

"Very," Gaby said. "We can't wait."

"I have five kids myself," Leslie said. "My husband wanted an even half dozen."

"Wow, that's like an army," I said.

"That's just what my husband said. He wanted a half dozen and to call them the Dune Platoon," Leslie elaborated, her last name apparently being Dune. "But I told him the only way that was going to happen was if he got pregnant himself."

I couldn't imagine having five kids and living in New York City. Piling five kids into a car was not the same as getting five kids onto a crowded subway. Just keeping them together would be a challenge. You were bound to lose at least one or two of them. The city was an urban jungle and required survival skills you wouldn't find in most places. To raise five kids in New York City, you'd need to equip them with tracking devices.

I left Gaby to talk to Leslie and wandered outside the room.

I walked through the corridor. Nothing seemed out of place, just the typical hospital feel—sterile with a medicinal smell. The hallways and corridors were filled with the normal hustle and bustle of any medical facility. Families were coming and going, and staff were doing what they always did, taking care of patients' needs.

I wandered out the revolving door of the maternity wing and walked down the hall. At the end, there was another glass door that led to an outdoor deck. I walked out to get some fresh air. After all that surreal activity and commotion that had been around me in Ashley's room, it felt good to get out.

There were a few scattered wooden lounge chairs on the deck. I stood at the railing and looked out onto the unfamiliar city. It all seemed so alien, not just the city of Shreveport but the reason we were there. It was as if I were living in a mind game from the movie *The Matrix*. It was hard to tell what was real and what wasn't.

"You know I'm not in favor of any of this."

I heard a stern voice from somewhere behind me. I turned. It was Sharon, standing in a corner of the deck, puffing away at a cigarette. I noticed the two spent cigarette butts near her left foot.

I didn't know how to answer that. I tried to smile.

"She's my daughter. She's stubborn, and once she makes up her mind, it's hard to convince her otherwise. I'm just hoping once she sees that baby, she'll change her mind."

Fuck you and mind your own business, I wanted to say, but I opted for, "Well, she's a grown woman, and I'm sure she knows what's best for her child."

Sharon walked toward me and rolled up the sleeve of her shirt even tighter. I was sure she was about to hit me. *Shit, maybe I said "fuck you" out loud.*

"See that?" Sharon said, pointing to a tattoo that looked like a baby's face. "That's my grandbaby Beau after he was born. And this one." She pointed to another one of her many tattoos on the other arm, this one with just a name: Beau. Sharon then turned her arm palm up. There was another tattoo: Mickey Mouse. "Beau loves Mickey," she added.

You know that's copyrighted, I thought. *You're fucking breaking the law. I'm calling Disney.*

"I know you mean well, and you seem like a nice couple," Sharon went on. "But let me tell you something. I don't care how much money you got to buy yourself my baby. No blood kin of mine is gonna end up with strangers in some liberal hellhole like New York City. Got that?" Sharon tossed down the cigarette, stomped on it with the tip of her worn, dirty sneaker, and then walked away.

"Nice talk!" I said as I watched her open the door. I was dumbfounded.

Was this really happening? Blood kin? *What the fuck.*

And what was this about New York being a liberal hellhole?

There was another, smaller, very disturbing tattoo on her shoulder, nearly hidden by her shirt. I saw only part of it, and I couldn't be 100 percent sure, but I think it was a swastika.

I hated to think what Sharon would have said if she knew I was Jewish. Maybe Sharon and Ashley had never even seen a Jew in person. I made a mental note that when this was all over, I'd send her a picture of me wearing a yarmulke, holding the baby.

One thing was clear, though: Sharon was our nemesis. That chain-smoking, narrow-minded, piss-poor excuse for a grandmother had declared war on us, and I wasn't going to take it lightly. Now more than ever, I wanted that baby. That little girl didn't deserve to be around someone so toxic. The secondhand smoke emanating from that woman was grounds for an accusation of child abuse in itself.

But I couldn't let Gaby find out about my conversation with Sharon—at least not now. Gaby was flying toward an unimpeded happy ending. She didn't need to know about Sharon, the backwater Cruella De Vil who wanted to make our lives miserable. I wasn't going to let that happen. The script was still being written; the ending belonged to no one. Now I was more determined than ever. Sharon gave me the one thing I needed to take this to a whole other level: hate. Yes, that eye-of-the-tiger, laser-focused, one-dimensional kind of hate. I'd seen my enemy, and she was going down.

I returned to the room. Gaby was chatting comfortably, bonding with the nurses. Sharon was with her daughter behind the curtain. All I could do was wait for the labor to begin. Hours, they said.

I sat on a chair. I just needed to close my eyes for a few minutes, to escape and clear my head.

"Wake up," Gaby said, touching my shoulder. I opened my eyes, at first not certain where I was. I looked at all the action around me. More people were in the room.

"I must have dozed off," I said.

"I'll say," Gaby said. "Almost three hours. We're starting."

I quickly stood, getting my bearings. Gaby was wearing a surgical mask and disposable hospital robe.

"Here, put this on," she said, handing me a similar mask and cloth robe to wear over my street clothes. I realized we were going to be present for the delivery. That had never been discussed. I figured we'd just show up, wait nearby, and once it was over, walk in and get the baby. Being in the room for the actual delivery wasn't on my agenda. I didn't need to see that. *Fuck, no!*

I knew that was what fathers did. They stayed for the delivery to watch their child enter this world. They wanted to see that little being they had been awaiting for the past nine months emerge from Mommy. The relief and satisfaction must be enormous for a dad. But there was something phony to me about us being there. We had just arrived on a plane. It felt to me like we had just showed up for the last play of a championship football game after being absent the entire season. We didn't belong there.

Ashley remained behind the partially opened curtain with the doctor, another nurse, and Sharon. I became fidgety, anxious, like a trapped animal while a hunter approached for the kill. I started to pace back and forth. I needed to leave, even though I knew that staying and being present for the birth would make me closer to the baby who would soon emerge. I inched my way toward the door.

Gaby and Leslie were standing outside the curtain near the opening. Leslie was treating Gaby like the real mother, and Gaby was buying into it all. After all, she was there to take the baby, to be the mom—the only mother that the baby would ever know. I was the phony one.

"You're getting there," Dr. Groda said from behind the curtain.

Leslie smiled at Gaby, indicating that the baby would soon be there.

What was I going to do? I was stuck, a prisoner of a maternity ward, a fearful father-to-be—or perhaps not-to-be? Just then Sharon opened the curtain further. Scowling, she glanced at me briefly and left the room. She was not happy. What was going on? Was something wrong with the baby, with Ashley? I could now see Ashley with her legs up in the stirrups, ready to go. I turned away for a moment. Dr. Groda then appeared through the opening of the curtain.

"Gaby," Dr. Groda said under her mask, "Ashley wants you in here with her."

Gaby looked at me with the most glorious smile on her face. She pulled her mask up over her mouth and nose, and then she followed Dr. Groda toward the bed. The curtain closed behind them.

Yes! It was a victory for us! Sharon wasn't wanted. I let out a big sigh of relief knowing she had gone. Now I wanted to stay. I was okay. We were all going to be okay. The devil had left the room.

I stood near Leslie, waiting as the number ten was called out. And then I heard Dr. Groda yell, "Push! Push!"

That was followed by a few groans from Ashley.

I watched the curtains, as if the great and magnificent Oz stood behind them, ready to bestow wondrous gifts on his loyal subjects.

"Push!" I heard again.

Then I heard the most wonderful sound of all, a newborn baby's cry.

Leslie was holding a white sheet as she waited outside the curtain. Dr. Groda walked out holding the tiny, crying baby and handed her to Leslie, who quickly wrapped the baby in the comfort of the soft, billowy sheet. Gaby was Leslie's shadow and followed her to the neonatal station that was set up near the window. I watched.

Dr. Groda lowered her mask and then smiled at me. "You have a healthy little girl."

"Oh, wow," were the most intelligent words I could muster.

I felt relief and exhaustion after a hard-won battle. I had a girl? But I had done nothing. I was being treated like I was the birth dad, and all I had to do was stand there. Is that how it was done? The adoptive parents become the parents that quickly? *Okay, it's over. Can we go now?* I wished it were that easy, but I knew only the first battle was over.

Everyone had told us that the less contact Ashley or anyone else in the family had with the baby, the better. The easier it would be for them to let go. And the quicker we held her and bonded, the quicker she'd be ours.

"What's her name?" Dr. Groda asked.

"I'm not sure. I think Gaby mentioned that she liked Chloe." I seemed to recall that name from our experience with Amber.

"Great name. I have delivered several Chloes," Dr. Groda said. "Enjoy her."

I must have looked stupefied.

"I know it's a little shocking at first," Dr. Groda added. "But believe me, she'll grow on you. They always do. I have some more on their way into this world today. See you later."

"Thank you," I said as I watched the doctor leave the room.

Ashley was still behind the closed curtain. I made my way to Gaby and Leslie. The baby was being cleaned and prepared for her very first day. I watched Gaby. She couldn't take her eyes off the baby. She had the look of love at first sight. Even with her mask on, her eyes shone with the light of an enraptured soul.

The baby was carefully dressed in a tiny pink gown. Socks had been placed on her angelic feet. She was then wrapped in a soft white blanket and handed to Gaby. And just like that, Gaby was Chloe's mother. She had been a mom in her mind before all of this, but now that she was holding the baby, it was official.

For a moment, I too was lost in all of the euphoria of the beginning of a life, one that you will help shape and will be with you until the end of your days. It was a breathtaking moment. Gaby held the baby as if she were about to break, then gradually held her closer and closer, relaxing so naturally into those first moments of motherhood.

"Do you want to hold her?" Gaby asked me.

"Maybe later," I said.

For me, the euphoria was fading into harsh reality: the reality of a hostile grandmother and an impressionable, emotional birth mom behind the curtain. I was afraid to hold this gorgeous, precious little girl, afraid to get closer. We had to wait the rest of today, plus five full days, before she was legally ours, and I had a gut feeling we were going to have a fight on our hands, and this beautiful child was the prize we were fighting for. If there was going to be a battle, we weren't going down easy. But nothing was certain here.

"Chloe," I heard Gaby say for the first time. "You're so pretty. Yes, you are." Gaby looked up at me and smiled, officially confirming the baby's name. Hooray, I had gotten it right.

CHAPTER 23

In Limbo

WE LEFT THE HOSPITAL AFTER CHLOE WAS taken to the neonatal-care ward and Ashley was wheeled up to another room. The two of them should have no further contact. Ashley knew the rules: what was best for her baby, what was best for the adoption.

Gaby or the nursing staff would be doing all the feedings. Chloe was scheduled for her first feeding in a few hours. We had a lot to do before then.

"I'm so glad it's going well," Stacy said as I filled her in over the phone on details of the hospital and the birth. Gaby and I were in a Walmart. We talked as I pushed one of two shopping carts. Gaby filled them with stuff for the baby: blankets, formula, diapers, clothing, BPA-free baby bottles (who knew back then about BPA-free?) and on and on. So much shit to buy. It was like one of those game shows where you have only so much time to buy as much crap as possible. With the rate at which our carts were filling up, we were winning.

"And be sure you touch base with Boyd Jargas," Stacy reminded me. "Call him as soon as you can."

"All right, we will," I replied. Boyd was the local attorney in Shreveport. Adoption attorneys always worked with local attorneys unless the adoption was in the same state that you lived in. Each state has different laws. Making that transition from birth to adoption was always a challenge, but a network of adoption lawyers working together tried to make the process as hassle-free as possible.

As soon as I got off the phone with Stacy, I tapped Boyd's number. Gaby continued to fill the carts as I pushed. For her the adoption was already a done deal. She had held the baby—she had held her child.

"Great, they've got it!" Gaby said. I turned to her as she picked up a baby car seat. "This is the one *Consumer Reports* gave the highest rating for child safety."

When it came to getting what was best for our house, our lives, and now our baby, Gaby did her research. I knew she had it all mapped out. From the crib waiting in our house back in New York to the brand of tush wipes, all were ranked the best.

"Great," I said as Boyd's phone began to ring.

"Hello, this is Boyd Jargas," the voice answered. He had the kind of Southern accent that sounded like it belonged to someone who wrestled alligators for fun.

"Hi, Boyd," I replied. "This is Michael King. Stacy told me to give you a call."

"How are you, Michael?" Boyd said. "It's my personal pleasure to welcome you folks to our great city."

Boyd filled me in on the details of how things would proceed. When she was ready to be discharged from the hospital, Ashley would sign papers turning the baby over to us. (Chloe, I had to keep reminding myself. The baby's name was Chloe.)

"I'm partial to Chloe, by the way. That's my granddaughter's name," Boyd interjected in a side note.

"Gaby picked it," I said.

"A beautiful name," Boyd added, and then went on with his legal revelations.

Since Chloe had been born on a Tuesday, the mandatory five-day waiting period would begin tomorrow, on Wednesday. Although legally the process would not be finalized for five days, we could pick up the baby before that: usually around forty-eight to seventy-two hours after birth. If all went well, the signed surrender papers would be filed, and Chloe would legally be ours on Monday.

It sounded so simple, just a few more steps, like the simplest of homework assignments that were assigned at the end of senior year—more as a formality than for a grade.

I wanted to say something to Boyd about Sharon and the threat she posed. I wanted his feedback. Maybe he already knew about her. But I couldn't say anything within earshot of Gaby. She trusted that I was taking care of the details while she wallowed in the joy of shopping for her baby. She didn't need the additional stress.

Boyd gave me information about Sandy, another person who was now on our payroll. Sandy was the local social worker assigned to Ashley's case. States were always protective, as they should be, about the welfare of the BM. The expertise of a social worker like Sandy was required by the state of Louisiana in order to ensure that Ashley was comfortable with her decision. Adoption was a difficult process for the birth mother, and Sandy would be there to help her through it all. She would also act as a liaison between Ashley and Gaby and me, in case there were questions that any of us needed to be answered.

I parked the cart behind Gaby as she stopped to look over some items.

"I really appreciate your helping us," I said to Boyd as he wrapped up his overview of the next several days.

"Thank you, Boyd!" Gaby said loud enough for him to hear.

"Right back at you both," Boyd replied. "And you both feel free to call me anytime. I'm here for you. I mean anytime, day or night," he added in a way that made me feel that he really meant it. "Take care, now."

"You, too, and thank you," I answered, and then put the cellphone back in my pocket.

"He's such a nice guy, isn't he?" Gaby said, looking at the label of some baby product.

"He sure is. You talked to him before?"

"Briefly, before we came down," Gaby revealed. "Stacy suggested it. She said that it wasn't a bad idea to establish a rapport with him."

"I'm glad I'm in the loop," I said.

"I did it for you," Gaby said as she gave me a happy peck on the cheek. "I just wanted to make sure he was someone you'd trust and feel confident about. You know how you get if you think someone is a hard-blow."

"That's a 'blowhard,' sweetheart."

"Blowhard?" Gaby said, and then blew out a breath of air. "Like that? I don't get it."

"It's just an expression."

I could see she was making a mental note not to make that mistake again, but I knew she would.

"Well, we're almost done," Gaby said.

I looked at our two shopping carts. Both were nearly filled to capacity.

It took nearly fifteen minutes for the sales associate to add up all our items. "That's $696.69," the saleswoman said.

I handed her the credit card, thinking that was a rather odd number. There were a lot of sixes in that number. Weren't sixes supposed to be bad luck? *But I think they have to be all in a row.*

We brought everything over to our new hotel and checked in to room 112, a two-bedroom suite. It had been recommended by one of the nurses as a place that other adoptive parents had liked.

It would be Chloe and Gaby's home for at least a week until they could travel. Stacy was working on arranging a 24/7 nanny to move into the other bedroom to help Gaby with the transition to motherhood. Everything was nearly ready. We just needed to get the baby. It was all coming into place.

We returned to the hospital at around 3:30 in the afternoon. We were told at the nurses' station that Ashley had been moved to a different room. We stopped by her room to say hello before Gaby went to the nursery to see Chloe for her afternoon feeding.

We heard voices and laughter as we approached the room and

stopped at the door, dead in our tracks, as if the emergency brake on our car had been activated. Ashley had visitors. Sharon stood at the bedside next to a little boy about seven years old. I assumed it was Beau, Ashley's son. But the visitor we were most surprised to see rested in Ashley's arms—baby Chloe. Ashley was feeding her with a bottle. We could hear Chloe's sucking sounds.

What the . . . !

I looked at Gaby. Her mouth was open, and I could see the blood drain from her face.

"Hey, there!" Ashley said, spotting us as if we were welcome guests at her picnic.

"Hi, Ashley," I replied uneasily.

Gaby remained silent as we walked into the room and toward the bed. Sharon turned toward me. She had a smirk on her face. I wished I had Harry Potter powers and could "poof" her away to Israel's most Orthodox neighborhood. Let them deal with her swastika.

"What's going on, Ashley?" Gaby asked in a tone that said, *What the fuck?*

"I just couldn't resist," Ashley said. "Here." She handed the baby to Gaby. "I just wanted to get a good look at her."

Gaby took Chloe.

"She's the cutest, isn't she?" Sharon added, still smirking.

Gaby went to a green lounge chair in the corner of the room, sat down, and started to feed Chloe.

"Hello. You must be Beau," I said as I looked down at the adorable, sweet-looking little red-haired boy. "I'm Michael," I added, offering my hand.

Beau wasn't interested. "My mee-maw says you are taking my baby sister, Bonnie Blue, away from us." Beau said this with way too much hostility for someone his age.

"Momma, I told you I won't have none of that," Ashley chided Sharon. "Now take Beau out of here."

Bonnie Blue? That deserved another "what the fuck." Who were these people, plantation owners? That name sounded like something out of *Gone with the Wind*. Bonnie Blue was an even worse name than Elphaba.

"Come on, sweet bear," Sharon said as she took Beau's hand.

"Nice meeting you, Beau," I added, realizing that it was possible to dislike some children. I wished I could "poof" them both to the Promised Land.

Sharon and Beau left the room. Gaby remained seated on the lounge chair, focused adoringly on Chloe. I hoped she was so intently focused that the conversation had gone right over her head.

"It's my fault," Ashley explained. "I shouldn't have had the baby brought to the room, especially with those two around."

I didn't know what to say. I tried for honesty.

"I know this isn't easy for you, Ashley, or for any of us. But I want you to know how grateful Gaby and I are for your letting us be a part of your baby's life."

Ashley smiled, and I could see the tears in her eyes. I couldn't imagine what she was going through, the painful decision she was making, and how it must have been ripping her apart. She had just brought a life into this world, a world that hadn't been that great for her. And now she had to grapple with the reality that perhaps that life would be better off somewhere else.

Were we the best path for Chloe? Would she be better off with us than with her birth mom, the one who gave her life? Sure, Chloe would be given more opportunities. But was that always best? Struggle creates a stronger character—and maybe, in the end, that person would be better off because of it, maybe contribute more to this world. No one could know for sure. Chloe would probably have a better chance with us. Still, it was all a crapshoot in the end. Wasn't it?

"Thank you," Ashley said, wiping her tears with a tissue. "I know what I'm doing is best for Bonnie Blue—that's what I call her; I hope you don't mind? If I had a girl, I always wanted to name her that—you know, the baby from *Gone with the Wind*? It's my favorite movie. I like it better than Chloe. Don't you?"

Are you out of your fucking mind?

"Bonnie Blue is a wonderful name. I'll mention it to Gaby."

My God, I was right. *Gone with the Wind.* I couldn't believe it.

"Bonnie Blue, no *fooking* way!" Gaby exclaimed as we stood on the outdoor deck of the hospital a little while later. "That's a horrible name. I don't care if it is a great movie!"

It was the same deck, but now I would have liked to push Sharon off. We had left Ashley's room shortly after the nurse picked up baby Chloe to take her back to the nursery.

"It's only for a while," I said. "And it's just a name. We'll call her whatever we want, but if Ashley thinks her child will be called Bonnie Blue and we get that baby, what's the difference?"

"They're making this a lot harder than it has to be, you know," Gaby said. "Everyone says keep the baby's contact with the birth mother to a minimum, if there's any at all! And what's with Beau saying 'my baby sister'? What's with that?"

So I guess Gaby had overheard my conversation.

"He's just a kid. I wouldn't worry about it," I said.

"Well, something is going on, and there's something about Sharon I don't like," Gaby added.

Something? How about everything? You don't know the half of it.

"Ashley seems to have her head together," I said, searching for something positive to say. "She knows what's best. She seems in control."

"I know. And I know how hard this is for her, but I'm starting to feel not so good about this."

"Come on, where's my always positive Frenchwoman?" I asked with a hint of sarcasm. She was more positive than most of the French people I had met. I mean, just look at some of those nihilistic French movies; they could drive Mary Poppins to suicide.

I wrapped my arm around Gaby's thin waist. "We're scheduled to bring her to the hotel soon. And then it's just a few days until she's ours."

Gaby looked at me. "You're right."

I squeezed her tighter and said, "This is a game. We've got a lot of players, and we just have to play along until we get what we want—and then it will all be worth it."

Gaby took a deep breath and smiled. "I love you," she said, and kissed me on the lips.

We walked back into the hospital and to the nursery for a last look at Chloe before we left for now; we planned to return that evening. She was asleep in her little plastic container, covered with the soft pink blanket with little pigs on it that Gaby had bought for her earlier that day. The name on her identification tag read BONNIE BLUE.

I knew then that this game was going to be harder than either of us could imagine. Monday couldn't arrive soon enough.

As we walked out of the hospital, planning to return that evening, I looked up at the cloudless, deep blue sky. I stopped for a moment to take in the beautiful day. *Dear God, give Ashley the strength to go through with it,* I prayed silently. *Give us the chance to be loving parents.*

We had a late lunch at a cozy, charming restaurant. Our waitress, Kim, was from Ohio, in her twenties, and she had a two-year-old girl at home. We chatted and Gaby told her why we had come to Louisiana. Gaby was never one to volunteer that kind of information, especially to strangers. But she needed to release some of the tension we both held. She needed to talk about it to a sympathetic stranger.

There seems to be a bond between parents of young children and parents-to-be. Having a child encompasses your entire world, so naturally parents are drawn like a magnet to people who are going through or about to go through the same things: diaper changes, sleepless nights, burp cloths, and witnessing the cute little things babies do every day. Oh, and worry, the constant worry.

I wasn't sure if it was cool to talk about the impending adoption. I was a bit superstitious that bringing it out in the open would somehow jinx the process. But maybe Gaby's way was better, to talk about it in a positive way, to put those good vibes out there to make it happen. When the outcome was uncertain and the stakes were so high, sometimes a little irrational thought might ease things along. It was okay to rely on the stars, a magic wand, good vibes, anything, if only it would help.

"I just know you guys will get the best baby in the world," Kim said as we were about to leave the restaurant. Gaby and Kim held hands as if they were old friends about to depart on their separate journeys. They embraced for a long moment. There was no need to say goodbye.

After lunch, we stopped back at the hotel to refresh ourselves, then returned to the hospital. It was becoming our routine: hospital, break, back to the hospital, repeat. The hospital was Grand Central, the hub of our little wheel: the headquarters that governed and controlled everything that was going on in our lives.

We arrived back at the hospital at about 6:30 p.m. We stopped first to look at the baby. Thank God, Chloe was sleeping in the nursery and was not with Ashley. By chance, Dr. Groda was doing her rounds and stopped to say hello.

I guess she could see the stress on our faces. "How are you folks holding up?" she asked as she smiled with compassion.

"Good," I said, not convincing even myself.

Gaby was more forthright. "I'm just a little worried that Ashley hasn't quite made up her mind."

"I don't have to tell you folks that none of this is easy," Dr. Groda went on. "It never is, especially for the birth mom. But I've known Ashley forever. She doesn't always make great choices, but she's not stupid. We've had long discussions about this. I know that girl, and there's no way she can handle raising another child."

Dr. Groda took Gaby's hand. "I think we're in a good place," she said, directly to Gaby. "And believe me, there's nothing I'd like more than to see you take that baby girl home." The doctor looked through the window of the nursery and saw Chloe. She shook her head.

"Bonnie Blue? I'll have to talk to her about that. See you tomorrow."

"Dr. Groda is so sweet," Gaby said. "I love her."

"Me, too," I said. "But she's not real—nobody's that nice, especially a doctor," I interjected, wishing but not quite believing that people like that were out there in the world.

"Relax, honey. You're not in New York anymore." Gaby touched my shoulder and smiled. Dr. Groda was the shot of adrenalin that Gaby needed, a boost to return her to her upbeat self.

We made our way to Ashley's room. Neither Sharon nor the demon child Beau was there. I relaxed. Things were looking good— except for the young man in the room, in his early twenties. Plump and a bit grungy, he wore an orange shirt and reminded me of a pumpkin. I didn't have to ask who he was.

Gaby put out her hand. "You must be Terry. So wonderful to finally meet you. Ashley has told me so much about you."

Terry took Gaby's hand but seemed too overwhelmed by her sudden greeting to reply. When Gaby hugged him and kissed him on both cheeks, he turned so red I thought he would faint.

"Nice meeting you," I said, holding out my hand. Terry took it without a word. His grip was loose and uncommitted.

Gaby moved to Ashley, and I was left standing next to Terry. It felt like we were actors in some kind of improv group, moving around the stage on cue.

Making small talk, I said, "I like your city. It's very nice."

"Not like New York City, I bet," Terry finally said. "Someday I'd like to get out there for work."

"What kind of work do you do?" I asked in what seemed like a setup.

"Well, I work at a car wash not far from here, but I'm really working on being a deejay," Terry said. "It's just going a little slower than I'd like since the operation."

I wasn't quite sure why, but I really didn't want to ask the next question.

"What kind of operation?"

"Brain surgery," Terry answered. "I had some kind of nose infection, and it went to my brain. They had to remove some of that gray matter stuff."

What do you say to someone who has just said that? *That must have been one hell of a nose infection.*

For the next half hour I heard pretty much Terry's entire life story: how he dropped out of high school to become a deejay, got his infection, was now making eight dollars an hour at the car wash, and didn't think much one way or another about being a father.

"Radio WCMJ, 1140 on your dial," Terry blurted out, his voice suddenly lowered into deejay mode. "It's the Terry Reynolds show, the Green City's go-to station for sounds that will rock your soul." He smiled. "What do you think?"

I didn't realize I was part of an audition. He smiled even more broadly as if he was waiting for applause.

"Wow," I said. "My God. I thought there was a radio on!"

"I knew it." He turned to Ashley. "Hear that, Ash? He said great stuff. And he's from New York City."

"Great," Ashley answered, not caring or paying attention to what Terry had just said. She continued her conversation with Gaby.

"Self-taught—there's no stopping me," Terry praised himself.

Except you live at home, got your girlfriend pregnant, and you had a quarter of your brain removed. Other than that, you're good to go.

I wished I weren't there. It felt like I was attending a fundraiser: first the sob stories to show you how nose infections kill or maim thousands every year, followed by a request for donations so no one else has to suffer like Terry did. Finally there was the celebrity to make everyone feel special. The only thing that was missing was the donation part. Maybe that was next.

I couldn't help but think about all of the fucked-up lives in the world. Still, living in the basement of your parents' house with your girlfriend and her daughter, I was certain, wasn't anywhere near the bottom of how bad life could be.

"It seemed you guys hit it off. That's good," Gaby said to me as we drove back to our hotel. She was animated and upbeat after her visit with Ashley, more certain than ever that soon we would be parents to Chloe.

"Yeah, he was a nice guy. Did you know he almost died from a brain infection that started in his nose?"

"I know; Ashley told me all about it. It was terrible. He was really sick for a long time."

Somehow I felt that Terry's life wouldn't have been much different one way or another. Now he had an excuse for his life being so messed up. How long did he wait to get that infection treated? Weeks? Months? Until pus started leaking out of his nose?

What's wrong with me? Why can't I be more sympathetic?

CHAPTER 24

Sucker Punch

WE SAT IN A BUSY RESTAURANT, waiting to place our order for dinner. As I watched those around us, it confirmed things I already knew: that people are the same no matter where you go. We all had the same needs that governed our lives and how we reacted to the world. The need to feel loved and feel a sense of belonging was universal, even if we knew it was transient or not real. At least it was something for now. Maybe this whole place, the transition that was about to happen, was somehow making me more philosophical. I felt I was about to embark on some incredible journey, and being more introspective was part of it.

That night, Gaby fell right to sleep without a worry. My mind raced for what seemed like an eternity, and then right before I fell asleep I realized that in a few days it would be Father's Day. *My God*, I thought. *My very first Father's Day!*

Wednesday morning at 7:30 our phone rang.

"Fuck!" I said. "Give us a break. This can't be happening again."

Gaby got to the phone before I did. It was Stacy, and within just a few words of conversation Gaby was already looking pissed.

"What's *wrong* with these people?" she exclaimed. "I know. I know that. All right. Yes, I realize that. I will. Thank you for calling."

I was already sitting up in bed as Gaby hung up the phone. I knew it wasn't good news.

Gaby looked devastated. "It's off."

"What are you talking about?" I asked. I expected bad news, but not that bad.

"Stacy just got off the phone with Boyd." Gaby's eyes welled up with tears as she spoke. "He said Ashley was really having a tough time. She went to look at the baby again and started holding her, and now she says she just can't go through with it. Shit, she could have told us that yesterday instead of putting us through all this."

"Fuck her!" I said as I sprang off the bed. "Fuck her mother! Fuck it all! Let's get out of here!"

Gaby just stared straight ahead. She was taking it hard. I mean, one minute we were going to be parents and the next we weren't. The closer we got, the greater was the emotional investment. It was the closest we had ever been. The loss shocked us both to the core. I took Gaby in my arms.

"It's better this way, Gaby," I said. "I mean tomorrow or the next day—who knows how long they could have dragged this on? It wasn't meant to be, but one day it will be."

Again, I wished I believed that, but how many times could Gaby handle hearing "It wasn't meant to be" before she started to think it would never happen?

"I know, honey; I just don't get it," Gaby replied. "Why didn't Ashley just make up her mind? What's wrong with her? I know it's very difficult to give up a child, but decide, one way or the other, and let us move on!"

We packed silently, checked out of the hotel, and headed for the airport without a reservation. We were willing to spend any amount of money to get us out of town, away from it all, as soon as possible. We wanted to go home.

We were driving onto the airport access road when my phone rang. I looked at the caller ID. "It's Boyd," I said. "Now what?"

Gaby remained sad and silent. I put my phone on speaker, pulled over, and parked in the lot of the nearest gas station.

"Hello, Boyd," I said.

"How you folks holding up?" he asked.

"We're just tired."

"I know, it all can be very draining. Well, the latest is that Ashley wants to talk to Gaby."

"About what?" Gaby asked.

"Sandy, the social worker, is with her now. Ashley just wants to make sure you are the right mom for her daughter."

"I don't know what else I can say," Gaby said. "We talked for a long time yesterday. She seemed totally on board."

"And then what?" I interjected, before Boyd could speak. "Tomorrow she'll tell us goodbye again? And then again and again?"

"It's possible, and I'm not going to lie to you: it happens," Boyd said in a calm and empathetic Southern drawl. "But this back-and-forth is also very common. Sometimes the moms just need a little push, a little reassurance that their child will be taken care of."

"I don't trust her. I never did," I said, unable to calm down.

But Gaby was the voice of reason. "I'll talk to her. I would never want her to let us be the parents of her child without her feeling one hundred percent certain that we are the right choice. If she doesn't, then we aren't the parents for her."

I smiled at my wife. She was 101 percent right.

A half hour later we were back at the hospital. It's funny how you think you'll never see a place again, and then your circumstances change and you do. Maybe you visit an old friend, say your goodbyes, then see him again because you left something at his house and had to return to pick it up. Awkward! Except in our case the little something we left was a baby.

I waited in the lobby. Gaby bought flowers to take to Ashley. A nice touch. But I knew for Gaby it went much deeper. I could only guess, but the maternal love for a child must run deep, like an instinct, shared by all women. Gaby's kindness was an act of love for

the child she wanted and empathy for the mother who was sacrific-
ing so much.

I could only imagine what they said to each other, what words
Gaby chose to comfort Ashley, to make her feel safe and as certain as
possible: words with such impact that they would give Ashley the
strength to allow us to become Chloe's adoptive parents.

It's all worth it in the end was the mantra I kept repeating in my
mind. All those who had done this before us, who had experienced the
pressure of trying to adopt and then succeeded, kept telling us that. "It
was all worth it in the end."

Nearly an hour later, I looked up from the local newspaper I was
reading to see Gaby approaching. She was talking to another woman
and she had a smile on her face. I knew we were back in the game.

"Well, how did it go?" I asked anyway.

"Fine," Gaby said. "Just a little glitch."

"Glitch," another word that sounded much better when said with
a French accent.

A giant fucking glitch!

"This is Sandy," Gaby continued. "Ashley's social worker."

Ashley's social worker? Shouldn't she be our social worker? I mean,
we were paying the bills. Didn't we at least deserve an "our"?

"A pleasure to finally meet you," I said, smiling at the attractive
pale brunette with a poufy, eighties-style hairdo.

Sandy shook my outstretched hand. "Likewise. I've heard so much
about you. I'm so glad things are back on track," she added. "It's very
emotional for the birth mom. I know one adoptive mother, a single
mom, who got rejected by birth moms seven times before she was able
to adopt."

"Well, that's encouraging," I said sarcastically, then realized immediately that I should have kept my mouth shut.

I got it: perseverance, don't give up, and all that. Positive was one
thing, but we didn't need to hear those depressing adoption stories

again and again. Five, seven, how about an even dozen tries? They finally got a baby, but by then they were bankrupt and couldn't afford to keep her.

"It requires a lot of patience and a little bit of luck," Sandy said, and smiled.

I knew I wasn't the first cynic she had dealt with. It all boiled down to a little bit of luck. This was still the most sensible summation I had heard since we started all this.

Still, there was something I didn't quite trust about Sandy. She talked almost exclusively about Ashley as if she were only *her* advocate. Sure, be supportive of the birth mom and make sure she understands her rights and decisions. I got that. Sandy was also there to reassure Ashley that we would be the most loving and supportive parents possible. In the end, it was all about the welfare of the child. So shouldn't Sandy advocate that the baby would be better off with us?

Wednesday brought no other surprises. We continued our culinary-distraction quest. That evening we went to a well-known Cajun restaurant. Dinner was a welcome diversion until the next afternoon, when the hospital was scheduled to release baby Chloe to us. We would take her with us. Tomorrow was a big day.

Our lives were not the only ones on hold. Not counting the patients whose appointments I had to cancel to make the trip, I estimated Ashley was influencing the lives of some sixteen people. All these people were focused on one common objective, to connect a birth mom to adoptive parents. Simple if everyone did their task. And it all depended on Ashley. The one person who in the past may have had little control of her life now had all the control. We were all on the same bus, but Ashley was in the driver's seat with her foot on the pedal. The success or failure of our mission was dependent on her final decision: yes, take my child; or no, she stays with me.

Gaby and I didn't even talk about it that night. We didn't want anything to jinx any of it. It was just silence and the hope in our hearts.

Chapter 25

Down for the Count

Thursday morning there were no phone calls that made our hearts skip a beat. The green lights were all lit and bright as ever. We set off to the hospital to pick up Chloe.

We arrived there around noon. Sandy was outside Ashley's room, talking to Dr. Groda. Just from their body language, I knew it wasn't good.

You've got to be shitting me!

I grabbed Gaby by the elbow to keep her steady. They turned to us as we walked toward them. They didn't look happy.

I looked briefly into the room. Terry, Sharon, and Beau stood around the bed. They were not focused on Ashley. They were all cooing over "Bonnie Blue" cuddled in Ashley's arms. Our world came crashing down again, without anyone uttering a word about its destruction.

"Fuck this. Fuck them all. Let's get out of here," I whispered to Gaby loud enough for anyone within five feet to hear. Where was my sympathy, my humanity? I was drained.

"We just found out about it ourselves," Dr. Groda said. She sounded pissed. "She's making a huge mistake. We tried. But we couldn't change her mind. I'm sorry."

We knew the score, but the finality of it was overwhelming. "Let's go," I said, taking Gaby's hand.

"Wait," Gaby said. She wasn't moving. "I understand. I can't imagine how she feels."

"She feels great," I said. "She got all this paid for, a cellphone, and . . . the baby. Of course, she feels fucking great!"

I knew I was being a schmuck. It didn't make me feel any better, but I didn't regret saying it.

"Michael, enough. Can I say goodbye?" Gaby asked, looking to Dr. Groda and Sandy. They both nodded.

"I think that would be nice. Regardless of what you think," Sandy said, looking at me, "Ashley feels terrible."

From Dr. Groda's expression, I could see that she didn't buy it either. I felt like we were being had. Gaby wiped away a few tears, put on a smile, and walked into the room.

Wow, she is such a better person than I could ever be.

Of course I was sad, but my anger overshadowed that. Gaby showed no bitterness, just deep sorrow, which she was able to put aside for the moment. She was an amazing woman, and at that moment I knew I didn't need anything else in this life except her.

I refused to go into the room. Sandy went in with Gaby. I wasn't sure why—maybe to act as a rational voice in case one was needed. I still didn't trust her. I felt she believed that, if at all possible, the birth mother should reconsider giving her child up for adoption.

I did trust Dr. Groda, who I now turned to. "I don't have to tell you this really sucks."

"I know. It always does," Dr. Groda said. "I've seen a lot of this after twenty-six years in this field, and unfortunately Ashley is near the top of my list of people who are not ready for a child, let alone two. I really am sorry."

"Thank you," I replied. "I wish it had turned out differently."

I saw Sharon turn to look at me while Gaby stood next to the bed. In response to her smirk that said, *I told you so, Jew boy,* I mentally flipped her the bird.

I watched Gaby talking to Ashley.

Don't pick up the baby, I kept thinking. *If you hold that baby again, it will only make it harder. Please, Gaby.*

I was relieved when she didn't.

Sharon, Beau, and Terry walked out of the room. I was sure they had left at Ashley's request. I guess Ashley felt she owed Gaby at least that, a final one-on-one.

Terry walked right past me without saying a word. Was it embarrassment, a lack of social skills, a loss of words (or brain) that caused such rudeness? I wasn't sure. Sharon walked out holding Beau's hand. We locked eyes.

"Come on, baby boy," she said to Beau. "We got to get the car seat for Bonnie Blue's trip home."

Bitch! How dare you be so insensitive?

I am normally not a hostile person, but I imagined putting a stake through her heart while I watched with joy as she evaporated like a vampire into a pool of sticky blood and body parts. Still, I managed to smile at her, which was so much harder than saying all the hostile words I wanted to say. She did not return the smile as she walked away. I was relieved that I would never have to see that woman again.

Soon Gaby returned. I hated seeing the tears and redness in her eyes. The pain went deep. We left the hospital and walked toward the car. The baby seat we'd brought for Chloe was in the back seat. Gaby was silent. I knew she needed to be alone with her thoughts. She didn't say anything until we pulled up to the hotel.

"You know she asked me if I wanted to hold the baby one last time? I thought that was insensitive. Am I being selfish? Should I have held her?"

"No, you absolutely DID the right thing," I answered. "Insensitive? I'd say. Why rub it in? Screw them all!"

"Maybe I asked for it by saying goodbye," Gaby said.

"Don't be ridiculous. You were a saint to that manipulating bitch. I'm sorry, but that's how I feel."

"At least I got to say goodbye. I wished her all the luck in the world and told her she'll be a great mom."

"You did the right thing. I know how hard it was for you. I'm so proud of you for doing that," I said as I tried to calm myself. But it was no use; my stomach was churning and calmness was hard to find amid so much anger.

I parked the car. We walked back to the hotel room in silence. Numbed by grief, Gaby sat on the edge of the chair. I turned on the television and sat on the corner of the bed. Together we watched the screen flash meaningless images that we hoped would dull our minds and our pain.

"Hungry?" I asked about an hour later.

"I guess so," Gaby replied.

We drove to a nearby sports bar. We got chicken sandwiches to go. We ate them back at the hotel room while we watched *Jimmy Kimmel Live!* Everything was an attempt at distraction, but nothing really worked. We tried to steer the conversation away from the hospital, the baby, and everything about why we were there.

My mind still raced thinking about the distasteful, insensitive, and tactless behavior of the entire birth family. Still, it would have been worse if we had actually taken the baby home and then this happened. Thank God for that.

We scheduled a flight out for early the next morning. We would have left that night if there had been a flight available. We were emotionally exhausted, but relieved that the gut-churning roller-coaster ride was over. Burned out, we both passed out on the bed with our clothes still on.

Early Friday morning was bright and warm, not a cloud in the sky. It didn't take long to pack. I was feeling a little better: not great, but a little better. I had rationalized that things probably worked out for the best—definitely a coping mechanism. Hadn't Ashley drunk, smoked, and who knows what else during her pregnancy? That couldn't have been good for the baby. And Sharon, the grandmother: there had to be some freaky genes in there. As for Terry, that was a whole other bizarre story, adding even more freaky genes to the baby's pool.

"There were a lot of loose screws with those people," I told Gaby as we drove toward the airport. "This maybe was a blessing in disguise." I focused on all the bad scenarios that could have been, hoping it would help Gaby feel a little better, at least for the moment.

"But Chloe—I feel so bad for her," Gaby said. "Right now, she's in some dismal-looking room. They weren't very neat. It's so sad."

And surrounded by smoke and a lot of other crap, I thought.

I should have just kept my mouth shut. In her mind, Gaby was still holding the baby in her arms. We pulled in to the airport and returned the rental car. The terminal wasn't crowded. The small, clean Louisiana airport was easy to maneuver as we made our way quickly through security. I think, in a way, the transition through security was a bit of an emotional cleansing process, separating us somehow from what we had gone through. We had crossed a barrier, and we were one step closer to getting back to New York City. We both relaxed a little more.

CHAPTER 26

Round Three

We had over an hour until our flight. Gaby settled into a chair near the gate while I made my way to the newsstand to buy the *New York Times*. That was when I felt the vibration. *It must be Richard.* He was one of those early risers who would often call me even before dawn to leave a message, even though he knew I'd be sleeping.

I looked at the caller ID. It was Stacy. I'd been too exhausted last night to call her—to let her know what had gone down. She had probably talked to Boyd, who gave her the bad news. She was calling to console us.

"Hi, Stacy," I said as I picked up the phone. "I guess you heard?"

"Yes, I did," Stacy replied. "Boyd called me last night, and then he called me again this morning. Chloe hasn't left the hospital yet."

"Why, can't they afford a car seat?" I said. It was over, and I didn't care about being nasty if it got me a chuckle.

"No," Stacy said. "That's not it. Ashley needed the night to think about what was best for her baby."

"Okay . . . ," I answered, not sure what was coming next.

"It seems that after Gaby said goodbye, Ashley realized what a great mother Gaby would be—how understanding and sympathetic she was, all qualities that would make her a great parent. She decided that placing the child with you both was the best thing."

"What the fuck!" I yelled out, and many heads turned toward me. "You know we're at the airport? We already checked in. If she thinks we're going there to go through this again—no way. We're leaving."

"I know how hard this is, believe me," Stacy said. "You can't imagine what some people go through."

She was wrong: I *could* imagine.

"And Ashley is aware of that," Stacy added. "She knows you don't trust her. That's why she signed the release and checked out of the hospital. You just need to go there and pick up your baby."

"You're shitting me!" I yelled, but now I was smiling.

"No, the baby is there if you want her."

I didn't have to think. I didn't have to ask Gaby. There was no debate—we were way beyond that. It was as though we were in a race, had stumbled and fallen multiple times, but somehow had managed to get back up and start running again. Bloodied and bruised, we were about to cross the finish line.

"Yes, we're on our way!" I said, and hung up the phone without waiting for a reply.

Gaby was reading French *Vogue* when I approached her. She didn't look up. I stood a few feet from her, hoping she would. Eventually she did. I looked at her and then grinned as wide as I could.

"What?" she asked, curious but a little annoyed.

"I just talked to Stacy."

Gaby sat up straight. "Why did she call?" I could detect a faint glimmer of hope in her voice.

"You must have said one hell of a goodbye yesterday. It convinced Ashley that you were going to be the best mom in the world."

"No!" Gaby said in disbelief, then stood up as if her shoes were spring-loaded.

"Yes," I replied.

"But they took her home."

"No, they didn't. Ashley and her family left, but Chloe's still at the hospital waiting for us. She's ours!"

The look on Gaby's face was the look of someone who had just been blessed by an angel. It was a look of pure bliss. We felt so much joy that it overwhelmed us. The child we had wanted so much would at last be ours. Tears came to my eyes as well.

It was a frantic hour. We had to wait to get our bags; then we rented another car and drove back to the hotel. I had given the hotel receptionist the baby stuff, and I hoped she was still on duty. Her name was Donna. She knew why we were in Louisiana, and she also knew why we had checked out. The hotel was near the hospital, and they were familiar with the process of adopting and the need for an interim home. Most of the time it worked out. Donna had seemed genuinely upset each time we checked out, knowing that it hadn't worked out for us. We had asked her to please give the brand-new car seat and bassinet to the next prospective adoptive parents who checked in to the hotel. She was still on duty. Just as she'd been two days earlier, she was elated to give it all back and to re-register us as long-term guests.

"I'm so happy for you both," Donna said.

"Thank you," I said, signing the registration card. I looked at Donna. She, too, had tears in her eyes. There was so much warmth and empathy all around us.

Finally we pulled up to the hospital entrance, and Gaby ran out of the car. We were too excited to waste time parking. Gaby would run in and get the baby; then we'd be on our way. I listened to music, tapped on the dashboard, stared at my fingers, then called my sister Andie, whom we had been keeping close in our emotional loop. Even though she had known others who had adopted children, this was family, and to hear firsthand the ordeal of the adoptive process sounded like a soap opera to her, with every episode ending in a cliffhanger.

"I'm so excited I could cry," Andie said, and she did. She was overwhelmed and elated that it was finally happening.

"I'll keep you posted. I have to go," I said hurriedly, too nervous to stay on the phone long.

I started to worry after a half hour had passed and I hadn't seen Gaby. Didn't Stacy say Chloe was ready for us to pick her up? "Here she is. Goodbye." Wasn't that all they had to do? Where were they?

Shit, something's wrong.

I was getting ready to call Gaby on my cellphone when I saw her coming toward the door in a wheelchair.

Something's happened to her!

But then I saw she was smiling, and I knew right away it was just hospital policy for new mothers. Sandy walked beside her. The wheelchair turned before I could see Gaby head-on along with baby Chloe being held in her mother's arms. Smiling, I almost leaped out of the car.

"I can't believe it! Look at her! She's so cute!" I yelled.

In an instant, my focus and my life changed. I guessed that was how it was supposed to happen when you have a child, no matter how you got there: the sole focus of your life became your child. Maybe instinct took over. Before this, there was doubt, resistance. But now, in her mother's arms, there was a baby, *our* baby. Something beyond description or definition took hold—something that only the experience of living it could teach you. In the space of one heartbeat, that baby was everything to me.

Gaby was beaming even more as the nurse wheeled the two of them closer to the car.

"Look at you both!" I said as I opened the back door.

The nurse gently took Chloe from Gaby's arms and attempted to secure the little bundle into the car seat, but it moved.

"It is not attached," the nurse said, almost scolding me as she took Chloe back into her arms.

"Oh, I'll get it." I moved quickly to fix it. "Sorry, I was so nervous—I forgot."

Forgot, my ass. I didn't know it required further attachments. I had just placed it on the back seat. Stupid! I fumbled with cords and hooks. I'm one of those guys with zero MacGyver skills. In fact, I'm the anti-MacGyver; instead of getting out of difficult situations, I make them harder. I thought you just put the baby in the car seat, threaded the belt around her, and off you went.

I was in panic mode as I tried to secure the damn thing. This had the same feel as kits of unassembled furniture: it seemed simple, but an hour later you're calling your friend with an engineering degree to come over and help you. (Then even he has difficulty getting the thing together.)

Shit! This can't be happening.

It was the endgame of some sinister plot where the last hurdle, the one you least expected, became your greatest obstacle. This was a test. If I failed they would take Chloe back into the hospital.

I expected the nurse to say at any moment, "I'm sorry, sir, but we can't release the child to you if you don't know how to install a car seat. What kind of father would you make? How can you raise a kid if you can't even do a stupid-ass thing like that?"

I could barely breathe. Something made me stop.

It's just a damn seat!

I tried to calm myself. I took a few seconds to appraise what I was doing, and then like a frantic, mad scientist, I just started attaching cords to hooks, hooks to cords, while pulling and tightening everything.

Two minutes later there was nothing left to tighten, pull, or attach. I was certain I had done it all wrong.

"I think I got it," I said, not really believing it.

Here it goes. It's over.

I moved back as the nurse checked my work. She tried to rock it back and forth, and it hardly wobbled.

"Okay," the nurse said.

The hospital was no longer accountable for the baby. Chloe was now officially our responsibility.

Ours!

"I'm so happy for you both," Sandy said, and seemed to breathe a sigh of relief. For the first time, I felt she was on our side.

"I'll come by the hotel on Monday," Sandy added as she gave a hug to Gaby.

"Thank you so much," Gaby said, getting out of the wheelchair with the help of the nurse.

Can you believe she just had a baby and she already lost all of that weight? I wanted to say, but kept my mouth shut.

I helped Gaby into the car. I ran around to the other side of the car like I was a contestant on *The Greatest Race* where time was of the essence. I just wanted to put as much distance as possible between the hospital and us, as if the greater the mileage, the more the baby would be ours. (I sped away at about three miles per hour, however, not wanting to disturb the baby from her sleep.)

Gaby was in the back seat with Chloe, staring at her and rubbing her little hand. Cars were honking at us from behind, and then as they passed us they honked again. I was certain the drivers were cursing under their breath and calling me the world's worst driver. Neither of us cared. If they'd known that we were first-time parents carrying the world's most precious cargo—our baby—home from the hospital, I'm sure they would have smiled and waved as they passed.

CHAPTER 27

Waiting for the Judges

A BLOND WOMAN WITH A CONTAGIOUS smile approached us in the lobby, pulling a small suitcase. "Hi! I'm Bobby," she said.

Although we hadn't met her, Boyd, the attorney, had arranged for her to be our temporary live-in nanny. He told us she was a divorced mother of two grown kids and would be a fantastic help.

We were easy to recognize. Gaby was carrying a bag of diapers, bottles, formula, even a blanket that came with the baby. It was part of the new-parent deal when you leave the hospital, sort of a goody bag for newborns. I was carrying the baby in her portable car seat, holding it with both hands like a bomb that was ready to explode.

"Let me help," Bobby said as she took Gaby's bag from her.

"I know it was last minute," Gaby said. "But we're so grateful that you were able to help us out."

From then on, every moment seemed to be a gift, like we were tuned in to a TV channel called Life Is Bliss. It was as if we were on a different plane of awareness where everything was simple and clear. We now had a baby to take care of, and that was all there was. Everything else in life was just bullshit. I had never had such clarity before. I felt enlightened.

We settled into our temporary home. Bobby got one of the adjoining rooms, while Gaby and I were in the other. The baby was in the shared living room space in the middle, in her little bassinet.

Everyone was so kind. It seemed to come with the territory of having a newborn. "Your baby is so cute." "Let me help you with that door." "Hello, little one, hello." Newborns spread contagious smiles and joy. If there were some way to bottle that, to keep that kindness around us all the time, the world would be a much better place.

My thoughts became mushy. A cynic by nature, I was now filled with the zeal expressed in the Beatles song *All You Need Is Love*. Love was everything, I thought, watching Gaby hold Chloe as she bottle-fed her the formula.

This was the role that fit Gaby perfectly, her destiny. This was where my Gaby seemed most fulfilled. She had always been a driven, successful, ambitious modern woman, but I had never seen her so content as she basked in the quiet grandeur of having a baby in her arms.

"You want to hold her?" Gaby asked.

"Me?" I said. "I don't think so."

I wasn't ready for that, not yet—maybe in a month or two. Holding a six-pound two-ounce fragile human scared me.

"Come on, honey," Gaby insisted.

I walked toward her. I figured I'd hold the baby for five seconds and then give her back, deed accomplished. I'd eventually work my way up to a minute or two in a few weeks.

Gaby put the baby in my arms. "Hold her head up like this," she said, demonstrating.

I held Chloe like I was holding a king cobra that was about to strike. Bobby and Gaby laughed together.

"No, like this," Gaby said as she brought the baby closer to me. Chloe's head rested in the nape of my neck.

I looked at her. She cried for a brief moment and then seemed to relax as if she had accepted my arms as her cradle. Her little hand grabbed my thumb and squeezed it.

How could this be, I thought? So much strength in such a little thing.

And then something happened. It was as if we had become joined. It felt like her strength became part of me. That is the only way I can explain it. I had a rush of emotion. I started to cry. All the hassles we had endured, the wars we had fought in the last few years, the battles to have a baby were over. We had won. The relief washed over me. It was the spark of love and it jolted an awakening in me.

"Are you okay, honey?" Gaby asked.

"Yes, I'm so okay."

Gaby and Bobby stared at me, as if they were watching another birth—the birth of a dad.

Friday night, in room 112 in a hotel in Louisiana, I became a father through and through. And I suddenly knew what all other dads had tried to explain but couldn't. It was a feeling so deep there were no words that could capture it fully. Some things just had to be experienced to be understood, and this was one of them.

Saturday we fell quickly into our new role as parents. Gaby and Bobby took care of Chloe while I ran errands. I made trips to the nearby Walmart to stock up on formula and diapers.

The itinerary of our new life was planned. I was to head back to New York early next week to see patients, and then I would return the following weekend. Gaby and Bobby would see to Chloe. In two weeks, when the baby was ready to travel, the four of us would drive back to New York City. Bobby would stay on as the nanny until we got someone local to replace her. Everything seemed perfect.

At Walmart, I grabbed an extra box of Similac baby formula. I knew we had plenty, but I didn't want them to run out of anything while I was gone. Overconsumption seemed to be the way of new dads, I thought as I saw another dad nearby, in his twenties, also piling up his shopping cart with baby things.

"How old is yours?" he asked.

"What?" I asked, a little confused.

"Your baby? How old is your baby?"

I could have kissed him on the lips. That younger man I had never met before questioned me as the dad, not the grandfather or the "Hey, too-old-to-have-a-kid guy," but as the actual dad. Maybe I had that new-father glow. Whatever it was, it made me so happy, like less of a fraud. I had passed and become a bona fide member of the "new dads club." I was okay.

"She's four days old."

"Wow, congratulations," the stranger replied.

"Thank you. How old is yours?" I asked, trying out the new-dad role and loving it.

"We have one of each. Our girl is five months and our boy is almost two."

"Two, wow. My first," I said, now beaming.

"Well, enjoy her," he said as he finished loading his cart. "I'll probably see you around—I seem to come here about every day."

"I hope so. See you soon," I replied. My first dad-to-dad bond.

How you came into parenthood seemed not to matter. We were just fathers doing what we were supposed to, taking care of our kids, nothing else. Chloe was Gaby's and my daughter, and how she got to be that seemed insignificant.

I didn't want that feeling to ever end. I closed my eyes for a moment in that aisle in Walmart, in a consumer canyon, surrounded by shelves piled high with consumer goods. I felt great.

I had no premonition of what was to come. I saw only a clear path to Monday, when the mandatory waiting period would be over and the papers would be filed. Stacy and Boyd would take care of the legal stuff, and Chloe would officially be ours. Emotionally she was ours already; we just needed it in writing, a mere formality. I couldn't see it ending any other way. The gods, the powers that be, the karmic forces of the universe would not allow otherwise.

Looking back on it, parts of it seem like a blur now. It was like being on the best vacation ever, or on a date that I never wanted to end. Each moment seemed better than the last. Breakfast, lunch, dinner, going to the bathroom were almost invisible necessities, brief pauses away from Chloe. She made everything else seem irrelevant. Picking up bread, getting change for the laundry machines, mundane things you did every day suddenly all had a bigger purpose. We were parents, working to make our child's life as good as we possibly could. There was no past or future; the now was all there was. Moment to moment with our child was all that we needed.

I had never had such a glorious feeling before.

And the rewards: wow, the rewards. When your baby looks at you (even though I'm sure I was a blur, a blob in her nascent mind), it was a look that said, "Hey, big person, I'm so glad you're here for me." It was a look that flooded my heart with joy. Any new parent must know that feeling, must know that nothing could ever replace that.

We talked to Stacy and Boyd on a conference call about how things would go. Come Monday after eleven a.m., all those little clauses in the legal documents, the ones that gave Ashley the option to renege, to change her mind, would become null and void. We just had to go to Boyd's office to sign some papers, he would file those papers with the court, and voilà, it would be a done deal.

The stories I'd heard about the old days, years ago, before adoptive parents had any rights, still lurked in my mind: instances where the birth mother or father would come back years after the adoption and try to get his or her child back. I couldn't even imagine the heartbreak, the hell some of those adoptive parents must have gone through.

Enough bad thoughts!

The rest of Saturday was filled with lots of phone calls to concerned friends and family to let them know how things were going. We felt confident that we were out of the closet of doubt and ready to break the news to the world.

"We got her! She's unbelievable! Things couldn't be better!" I went on and on, broadcasting the good news to my cousins, aunts, uncles, sister (who was beside herself), and, of course, to Richard.

"You did it, bro," he said. "Welcome to the world of constant fucking worry."

Gaby had similar conversations with her family and friends, only in French. Still, the tone of excitement felt the same.

Saturday night, Gaby and I went out for dinner at a popular Louisiana seafood restaurant. We didn't want to leave Chloe.

"You guys need a little time to yourself to unwind," Bobby insisted. "Don't worry, if I need you, I'll call."

"You sure?" Gaby asked.

"Yes, we'll be fine," Bobby said. "Go have fun."

And Bobby was right, alone time was just what we needed. We were exhausted—the kind of exhaustion you feel after you have been studying for college finals for a week and suddenly it's over. Such fatigue earned a well-deserved reward.

We sat in a comfortable wood-trimmed booth. We each ordered a glass of champagne.

"To Chloe," I toasted. "The best thing, other than getting married, we ever did."

"To our Chloe," Gabby added.

A clink of the glasses and a sip of champagne, followed by a kiss, was part of our romantic interlude. We were in love, content, and now a family. We couldn't ask for much more than that.

I slept so well that night. I heard the baby cry from time to time, but it was like music, the music of life, lulling me into an even deeper sleep. Gaby and Bobby alternated Chloe's feedings. They knew I wasn't comfortable with it all. Besides, Gaby wanted to bond. She wanted to be there as often as a biological mother would be. I felt only slightly guilty as I rolled over and went back to sleep, but I knew that soon enough, like all new dads, I would be sleep-deprived.

When I awoke on Sunday morning, for a moment I didn't know where I was. Gaby was sleeping next to me. Was it all a dream—were we really parents? I slipped out of bed without awakening Gaby from her sleep. I made my way into the living room between the two bedrooms. I saw Bobby on the couch, sleeping. I walked to the bassinet and looked down. It was all true. It had been confirmed: there was really a baby here.

Baby Chloe was snuggled into her bassinet, sound asleep. I just stared at her. Strange—usually when I looked at a child, it was fleeting: a mom strolling by with her baby, kids playing in a park, or watching my nephews swim. I'd probably watched them in their cribs years ago, though I couldn't remember it now. But this was different. This baby wasn't going anywhere. It was that permanence that caused me to look with different eyes—eyes that belonged to a dad. Eyes that were telling my brain, *This baby is yours. Enjoy.*

"She looks just like you," whispered a voice, and I turned to see Bobby standing behind me.

"Yeah, right," seemed to be the right thing to say.

"Really, she has your same color complexion."

"Poor kid, she's going to be pale her whole life."

"I've seen it before with other adoptions," Bobby elaborated, "when one of the parents looks like the baby. It's amazing, like it was meant to be."

And there it was again, what I heard over and over from people I had met on this journey, "It was meant to be." Bobby was convinced. I didn't believe her, of course.

Absurd. That's impossible.

But something compelled me to stare at Chloe harder. I wanted to believe it. I wanted to see the resemblance as if this were preordained: a divine happenstance, somehow orchestrated by the powers that be. Chloe, as if on cue, suddenly opened her eyes and looked right at me.

"See, she already knows you," Bobby added, making her case. "Look at that smile."

It was really more of a smirk, I thought. But she was looking right at me. Yes, at her dad.

"Hi, Chloe. Little Chloe, how are you, sweetheart?" I said, smiling back at her.

And in that moment, I believed. I believed in heaven and hell, and that free will was nonsense. Our baby was what God had willed. She was divine and was brought to us on the wings of an angel.

I turned to Bobby and smiled. "Do you really think she looks like me?"

"I know it," Bobby replied.

Chloe closed her eyes, and I continued to stare at her as if she were surrounded by an aura of peace.

CHAPTER 28

KO'd

LATER THAT MORNING, AFTER GABY FED THE BABY, the four of us strolled toward the hotel dining area for breakfast. Gaby pushed the stroller. It felt like we were a military unit. Everyone had their task, and now we were marching toward grub.

Everything was working out. It was all too good to be true. I didn't want to think about those other possibilities, the bad ones. I tried to put them out of my mind.

Tomorrow's the big day.

After that, there would be no more worries and none of that constant, nagging tension.

Neither Gaby nor I mentioned the tension. I thought we were pretty good at hiding it. But it was there; too much was at stake. Each second, each minute, Chloe grew closer to us, deeper in our hearts, becoming part of us—becoming our family.

Staying focused and positive was all I wanted to do that day. No contact with family and friends. It was all too visceral, too soulful to include anyone else right now.

We were all having breakfast *al fresco*. The temperature was perfect. We sat on the patio under a large umbrella. The phone would vibrate with nonstop calls from my cousin, my sister, my aunt, Gaby's stepmom and dad, and Richard. We didn't pick up; we would call them back when we had certainty.

Then I felt another vibration, another call I wasn't going to take.

Still, I glanced at the phone screen and my heart sank. It was Stacy. She wasn't supposed to call us until tomorrow. This couldn't be good. I could feel the blood rush out of my face. I wanted to hide, disappear, make the phone call go away. But I was being an alarmist. It was probably nothing. She forgot to tell us something.

Please, God, let it be that.

I took the call. "Hi, Stacy."

Gaby and Bobby stopped eating and just stared at me as if they had seen a ghost.

"Hi," Stacy said, and just from the way that one little word sounded, I knew it wasn't good. The soft, reluctant way she greeted me said it all.

I tried to hide what I was feeling, hoping to postpone even for one second what I knew was about to come.

"I just got off the phone with Boyd. Ashley changed her mind."

And there it was.

"No." I could barely speak.

"She's coming to pick up the baby," Stacy said.

"You're shitting me?" I said in disbelief.

Gaby's eyes were already tearing up, as were Bobby's and mine as well.

"How can she do this? Maybe she's just having second thoughts again?" I said, but I knew better.

"No, she's certain. Boyd is certain. She'll be there in about an hour," Stacy said, not trying to sugarcoat it or give us any false hope.

"Fuck!" I said.

Gaby quickly stood up and left the table, carrying the baby back into the hotel. Bobby went with her.

"I know how you feel, believe me," Stacy continued. "I've been through this more times than I want to remember. But this is a hard one. Harder than most. I'm so sorry, but there's nothing we can do. She still has all the rights."

"It's not fucking fair," I said.

"It never is," Stacy said.

"So that's it?" I asked.

"For now. But listen, I know you don't want to hear this now, but you have to believe there's another child out there, the one that was meant just for you guys."

But this was her.

This was the one who looked like me, who stared at me, who squeezed my finger so tight.

"The worst thing you could do now is give up," Stacy said. "Not after you've come so far. Just trust me on this."

Stacy was being what stereotypical lawyers seemed to avoid: human, heartfelt, speaking as a parent, as someone you could believe in. I trusted her completely. It was all that I had.

"Boyd said they'll be pulling up to the lobby entrance at about one p.m. I'm so sorry."

"All right, we'll have her ready."

Without another word, I ended the conversation. No good-byes, just nothing.

I sat there for a moment. This couldn't be happening. It felt like I had been stabbed in the heart. Someone had reached inside me and grabbed all the happiness I had and then crushed it to dust in their hands. It was over: no more deals or negotiations or changes of heart. The end had arrived and it was brutal.

I thought I'd find Gaby and Chloe in the lobby, but they weren't there. Maybe Gaby was doing what I'd thought about doing: fleeing, taking the baby and escaping, getting on a plane, flying to some foreign country that supported the kidnapping of children, and living out our lives as the family we were meant to be.

When I walked into the room, Bobby was feeding Chloe. The deep sorrow across her face said it all. I'm sure she had been through this before, but it was still painful for her. She too had fallen in love with Chloe. She knew this would be the last time she would feed her.

I tried to smile as I nodded.

"Where's Gaby?" I asked.

"In the bedroom," Bobby answered, not taking her eyes away from the baby.

I expected to see Gaby lying on the bed, sobbing. Instead, she was putting on her workout clothes.

"When are they coming?" she asked before I could say anything. I was concerned that there were no tears.

"In about an hour."

"I don't want to be here when they take her," Gaby said as she tied her running shoes. And then she started to cry. She couldn't hold it back any longer.

"I can't take it. I can't. It's not fair," Gaby said. I took her in my arms and held her as tight as I could. I could feel her tears dripping down my neck and I'm sure she could feel mine.

"I know, honey, I know. None of this is right," I said. "But you know what I also know?"

"What?"

"We're going to get a baby, another beautiful baby."

"I don't think I can go through it again," Gaby said.

"Look at me," I said as I held her away from me for a moment. Gaby looked at me. It was the look of someone who had just gotten the news that a loved one had died. Only our loved one was in the other room. Soon, just as with a death, she would no longer be with us.

"This isn't over. I'm certain," I continued. "We were so afraid at first, especially me. Now look at us. We are loving parents. We know the feeling. We've lived it. We couldn't have done it without Chloe. She was our test. Don't you see? Our test that we've got what it takes to be the best parents ever. To love a child like we could love no other. Chloe was our angel who came to rescue us. To show us what it's like to be parents. That's why she was with us. You have to believe it."

"I want to. I do . . . but what if it never happens?" Gaby asked.

"It will, I know it will. We will—whatever it takes, however long it takes—be parents. I promise you. And you know I never make promises I can't keep. Do I?"

"No, you don't," Gaby said.

"My love, we're here for a reason, and I'm a hundred fifty percent sure of it. And you know what I think? The third mom we meet will be the one: three's the charm."

"Really, you really think that?" Gaby asked.

"Absolutely!"

Gaby managed a smile through the tears and breathed a little easier.

As for me, I believed everything I said, except the part about three being the charm. I wasn't sure about that. But I was sure we'd find our child. I was certain it would happen one day. That feeling of being a dad, I wanted it more now than I had ever wanted anything in this world. I wanted it for Gaby, I wanted it for me, and I wanted it for the family we were meant to be. I didn't care how long it took, how much money it cost, or how we did it; I wanted that feeling again. And there wasn't anything in the world I wouldn't do to make that happen.

Our good-byes to Chloe were brief. Gaby held her in her arms and kissed her lovingly on the nose. She held Chloe tighter, her face next to hers. It was a mother's last embrace. As for me, I held her tiny hand again. "I hope you have a good life, little one. You could have had a Lexus and not some shitty old Toyota."

"Honey!" Gaby scolded me. But again, that was the Jewish way, finding the humor even under the worst possible circumstances.

The last thing Gaby did was wrap Chloe in the little pink blanket with pigs on it, the one she had brought to the hospital. "Please, give them everything else we bought for her—everything," Gaby instructed Bobby.

"I will," Bobby promised.

"Goodbye, my love," Gaby said, staring at Chloe for the last time. Then we left the room together.

CHAPTER 29

Throw In the Towel

GABY WENT TO THE GYM. SHE NEEDED the distraction of a workout, anything to take her mind away from the living hell we were in. As for me, I needed a long walk.

Fifty-two hours. I was a father for fifty-two hours.

I walked down the unfamiliar busy street, trying to forget, trying to take in the new sights: gas stations, mini malls, homes, and a school—but none of them registered.

Nearly an hour had passed when somehow I found myself back across the street from the hotel—maybe I had planned it unconsciously. But I saw what looked like a beat-up brown Corolla parked in front of the hotel. Bobby was by the open trunk, putting things inside. Sharon was helping. When they closed the trunk, I saw Ashley holding Chloe or whatever the hell she was calling her.

Ashley was the mother. She had brought the baby into this world and was holding her as any loving mother would. I knew that Chloe would be loved. Maybe that was all she needed. Maybe the statistics were wrong. Chloe would somehow rise above it all. She had that strong grip of a fighter. I had to believe she would.

I watched them put Chloe in the car seat. Ashley got into the back with her. Sharon got into the driver's seat and off they went. Sharon glanced at me as the car drove past. She didn't smile in triumph. At least I was glad about that.

When I went to the exercise room, Gaby was still running on the treadmill. She had the headphones on. I walked to where she could see me. She stopped the machine. I could see she had been crying.

"Are they gone?" she asked.

"Yes," I said with a nod.

"Please, take me home." Gaby wiped her eyes. I wiped mine and then remembered: today was Father's Day.

PART VI

BREATH OF AIR

CHAPTER 30

Mourning

FOR SEVERAL WEEKS AFTER WE GOT BACK, I seemed to lose all my sense of humor. I felt a kind of numbness inside. I was going through the motions, but nothing felt good or meaningful. It was as if the air were being removed from my body. Some days I could barely breathe. I looked in a mirror. I looked the same, except in the eyes. They told the truth. I was dying inside.

The image was so clear in my mind of that little one whom I had held so close. Images flashed before me of Gaby, caressing Chloe in her arms as she smiled like I had never seen my wife smile before—a smile of ultimate joy.

They took her away.

My nose had rested on her sweet head. She had the freshest of all smells: *eau de bébé,* the smell of hope and the future. And then it had ended. Boom—just like that—it was over.

They fucking took that away!

I didn't know what to do. Maybe I should see a doctor. Something was so wrong.

"You're depressed," Richard said to me one day. And he would know what he was talking about, since he occasionally suffered from depression himself.

Maybe he was right. I had never felt depressed before. I felt like I had entered some kind of hell and couldn't get out. I was doomed to live there forever.

Gaby seemed affected also. She seemed always glum, fake-smiling only for my benefit.

And then one day I was reading the obits in the *New York Times*, and it struck me. We were going through mourning. Losing Chloe was a death for us, and we needed time to grieve our loss.

CHAPTER 31

Hallie

I'M NOT CERTAIN WHEN IT HAPPENED. Maybe it was a month after we got back from Louisiana. But one day I woke up and everything seemed different. Everything had color and life again.

That night the same thing happened to Gaby. Maybe she sensed the change in me, and it helped her to move on. Or maybe partners in love sometimes move as one, their internal clocks in sync.

I was in the kitchen, making pasta for dinner, when Gaby came home from work.

"Hi, honey," she said in a tone I hadn't heard in a while. "How was your day?"

"Fine," I said. "Busy, lots of patients."

"Good," Gaby said, and she kissed me. "I want to be a mom again."

And that was all we needed. As if a weight had been lifted off our hearts, we felt liberated, alive for the first time in weeks. We had managed to pull ourselves out of the funk. We were back among the living.

"I was thinking about what you said to me in Louisiana," Gaby continued. "And you were right. We are meant to be parents. That was our test. Don't you want to be a dad again?"

I was overwhelmed. Words weren't enough. I smiled and picked up the phone and tapped a number. "Hi, Holly," I said. "It's Michael and Gaby." Two days later the ads were running again.

We were in it all over again. The screenings, the phone calls: everything was the same, but something was different. We were different. We knew exactly where this was going—it was leading us down the road to our child. We believed that without a doubt. We were going to get there this time.

We fielded, we talked, we passed. Nothing, nothing, nothing. Months passed. It was November when Gaby talked to Lynn.

Lynn was the hard-working single mother of a pregnant sixteen-year-old who was due to deliver in February. Gaby said the woman sounded great over the phone. Lynn had always been a single mom and didn't want the same thing for her daughter, Hallie, who was an A student in high school. Lynn wanted to give her daughter every opportunity that she hadn't had, to help her avoid going through all the struggles that she had. College and a career were goals she had set for Hallie, goals that would quickly be curtailed if Hallie had to take care of a child. Lynn just needed to find a home for the baby, a home that she was certain would be wonderful and loving.

The papers were filled out, medical reports sent, and our adoption album mailed off all in a matter of days. We were hopeful that this would be the one. The third one was the charm, right?

A week passed and we didn't hear back from Lynn.

Two weeks later, at dinner at our favorite New York restaurant, Cookshop, Gaby sprung it on me. "Cancel your patients on Saturday."

"What? Why would I do that?"

"We're going to Indiana. Lynn and Hallie want to meet us."

"You're shitting me?"

"No shitting," Gaby said.

Fort Wayne, Indiana, reminded me of how Denver looked and felt when I was a kid: like a small, manageable, and wholesome city.

We arrived in the early evening and checked in to our hotel, room 208. Seventy-one dollars a night for a room with a king-size bed and a view of the highway. How could they make a profit at that price? It boggled my mind. We then headed to Huntington, a cute little town about a half-hour drive from Fort Wayne.

It was 8:15 p.m. when we turned down the well-lit street of the solidly middle-class neighborhood. Most of the houses were two stories with white picket fences. It was a *Leave It to Beaver* neighborhood if I ever saw one. We looked for the right house and found it on the corner.

This couldn't be right, I reasoned to myself. This was a nice home: no trailer park or basement apartment or multifamily place.

"Are you sure this is the right address?" I asked Gaby.

"Yes," she said.

I made sure that my hair was slicked back. "You sure it's not too dark?"

"No, it's not," Gaby replied, knowing that my last dye job made me look like I worked in a coal mine.

"Sorry," I said, apologizing for my stupid vanity. I still tried to pull off the charade of looking ten years younger than I was, hung up on that too-old-to-adopt thing, even though I had no proof that it had ever mattered.

At the front door, as we waited for someone to answer, I puckered my lips several times in a row to tighten some of my facial muscles. Another exercise in futility.

"Please," was all Gaby said as she glanced at what I was doing. I realized it was a bit much even for a wife who was used to such things.

A pretty, blond woman in her mid- to late thirties answered the door, smiling.

Wow, she's so young to be a grandma, I thought.

"Lynn?" Gaby asked.

"Yes, please come in," the too-young grandma answered, her voice soft and sweet. We walked into the house.

"So glad to finally meet you in person," Gaby said as she hugged Lynn, followed by a peck on each cheek.

"And this is Hallie," Lynn replied, and Gaby and I turned toward the cute, petite blonde who walked toward us.

And there she was, the kind of birth mother most adoptive parents dreamed of: young, healthy, smart, beautiful, athletic, and from a good home. She was a good kid who had just made a mistake. This was the Holy Grail of adoptions.

And why would they pick us? Why?

But they did.

Three months later, there was one of the worst snowstorms the East Coast had seen in years. We were on a roll with the adoption process. After a few wrinkles at the beginning, the path had been cleared; the green lights were all lit. We had just gotten the call to go to Indiana. And then we got hit by the storm. It was a bad time for Hallie to go into labor.

We couldn't get out of New York City to be there for the birth. We tried so hard. All the flights were delayed—or worse, canceled. There was nothing to do but wait.

A day passed, and we were still stuck in New York.

Hallie gave birth. We couldn't be there.

We felt so helpless. We talked to Stacy almost every hour. Hallie had given birth to a healthy baby girl, and it was "still a go," according to Stacy.

"That's what she said," I reiterated. "It's *still a go.*"

"You're right," Gaby agreed, trying to be positive. "We're doing our best. Everything will be fine."

And then we got a flight, at last.

Then our takeoff was delayed again. Helpless and frustrated, we sat on the plane, waiting to finally make it to Indiana. Air travel was a mess as we waited for a break in the storm. This was the last flight out of New York for perhaps days, and the storm was just going to get worse. Gaby was nervous as she tapped the arm of the seat. She didn't want us to miss our connection in Atlanta. It was the long way around, for sure, but the only way we could get to Chicago and then to the connecting flight to Fort Wayne. What if we missed the connection?

After what had happened with Chloe, we were both worried about that. There were so many ifs. Wasn't there a limit on how long the baby could stay in the hospital? They couldn't take the baby home, not if she was going to be adopted. What if Hallie started to feed her, bond with her? We both knew that could be a disaster.

But we were determined, if only by sheer force of will, to make this one happen. It must.

We will get there in time to get our baby.

We had to believe that.

"This is your captain speaking. We have been cleared for takeoff."

I smiled at Gaby. Then the flight attendant got onto the speaker with the usual prep talk. And just like that, we were headed down the runway. As the plane lifted off into the night sky riddled with blinding snow, I squeezed Gaby's hand.

We pulled up to the hospital on a Saturday around one p.m. The weather had cleared and it was in the low fifties, a rather warm day for February. We were exhausted after the endless, sleepless plane journey consisting of two connections and riddled with leaden stress. I was unshaven and looked like I was hung over. Gaby looked beautiful even when she was tired.

We quickly parked the rental car and rushed toward the entrance of the hospital. Gaby moved with confidence, never wavering from her conviction that this was really the one, the baby we'd been waiting for.

I wasn't sure what we'd find. Was it still a go? It had been two days since the baby was born—two eternal days. As we both knew, a lot could change in two days.

When the elevator opened on the maternity floor, we walked into a nearly empty ward.

"Hello," Gaby said as she approached the nurses' station. "I'm Gaby and this is my husband, Michael. We're here for Hallie."

"Oh, hi. We were expecting you," the nurse said. She wore green scrubs under a blue lab coat. She had a warm smile. "The storm was pretty bad, I understand."

"Yes, it was, but we made it as soon as we could," Gaby said. *Where's the damn baby?*

"Hallie's in the lounge, second door on the left," the nurse said.

We walked down the hallway toward the lounge. The place was eerily quiet. We entered into a sunlit room with a green tiled floor and yellow-painted walls. Hallie was sitting on a recliner in the far corner of the room. In her arms she held the newborn baby. She smiled at us as we entered.

This is happening again. You've got to be kidding me!

Gaby looked at me, her face a shade paler than it had been a moment before, as if she was about to be sick. I wanted to turn around and run away, screaming, "No, not again!" But then Gaby, without hesitating, found her smile and walked toward Hallie and the baby. I held back. I already had my phone out and was tapping Stacy's number.

"She's feeding the baby," I said, trying not to sound stressed.

"It's fine," Stacy said. "It doesn't matter."

"What do you mean it doesn't matter?" I asked. "She's *feeding* her *baby*!"

"It doesn't matter," Stacy repeated. "In Indiana, once all the proper documents have been signed, notarized, and filed by the attorney, she's yours."

"What?" I asked in disbelief.

"It's done," Stacy said.

"How could this be?" I asked. "You're kidding me, right?"

"No," Stacy said, and I could feel the joy in her no. "You can take her home."

"Thank you," I said as I put the phone back in my pocket without even ending the call.

She's ours? She's really ours!

I looked at Gaby, Hallie, and the baby. Our baby! I watched Hallie gently hand the little girl to Gaby. She must have told Gaby that everything was finalized, that we could take the baby home. Gaby was smiling and crying. She looked at Hallie and then at me. My Gaby, my love, my wife, was now and forever a mom. I smiled and started to cry, too. I stood up straight and walked toward them with the confident stride of a proud father—a father at last.

Epilogue

I saw Richard recently for lunch. He has three grandchildren. He babysat for his three-year-old granddaughter the other day. "I was exhausted after being with her for an hour," he told me. "I'm too old for this shit. I could barely keep up with my kids twenty-five years ago. How in the fuck do you do it?"

"You just do it. I have no choice—and I use a lot of painkillers," I answered. "'Daddy, put me on your shoulders.' 'Let me take an Advil first.' 'Daddy, can we go rollerblading?' 'Sure, first let me shoot myself up with morphine.' 'Daddy, will you take me skiing?' 'Honey, I want to introduce you to your stunt dad.'"

Richard laughed at the absurdity of it all. Of course, he knew the answer: you do what you have to do, because you're a dad.

"Was it worth it?" he asked.

I do think about that now and then. All the shit we went through. The roller coaster of emotions. The stress—oh, the fucking stress. And the time, the waiting, the anxiety . . . how in the world did we do it? Were we fucking nuts? How does anyone do it?

The answer is, you just do. It's a battle we could have bailed out of at any time, and yet we stayed in the fight. If I had to do it over again, would I have started earlier? I don't know. You never know how things would have worked out. It's all a game. You play the best you can. And you make mistakes. Some mistakes cause pain that you never really get over. But that is all part of life, isn't it? It's one of many journeys we take. In the end, I hope the lessons I learned will make me a better person, for myself and for others.

If I could do it all over differently, I wouldn't have our Isabella. So no, I wouldn't change a thing. She is the biggest part of our lives. I still can't believe it. Sometimes it feels like a dream, a wonderful living dream. I feel so blessed. My child, she is so much a part of me. Like air, I breathe her in and out every second of my life.

Because of my age, I do worry about not being there for those essential parts of her life that will come later: marriage, children. What then? What about her?

Then I think, hey, this is life, that unpredictable thing we all do, trying to live and get by the best way we can. There are only odds, no guarantees. I hope I'm here for the long run, or at least long enough. But I realize now that what is important is not how long I live, but how I live. A moment of love is better than an endless life with no love at all.

So what if one day I move with a walker as I watch my daughter get her high school diploma? That walker can be customized with pin-stripes, a peace sign, and Day-Glo handles. I will be the coolest dad on a walker—a dad who will love his child fiercely till the very end.

"Was it worth it?" I repeated to Richard.

I smiled at him, thinking of what Isabella, who's four now, said to me the other night as I tucked her into bed. I was staring at her, like I so often do, marveling at the beauty of my child with her blond hair, hazel eyes, and precious smile. "Daddy, I love you like a shiny pie," she said, looking up at me.

"It's worth more than anything in the entire world," I told him.

THE BEGINNING

A Note to Prospective Parents

IF YOU ARE ON THE FENCE about becoming a parent, let me be the one to tell you to get off of it. Do whatever you have to do to experience the love that comes with having a child: get pregnant, adopt, have a surrogate baby, or foster a child.

Just don't steal one.

Being a parent is the single most rewarding experience in the universe. It's what life is all about.

And if you think the purpose of having a child is so you can enjoy a family, think again. That's the result. The real purpose goes much deeper than that. The purpose of having a child is so you can teach that child how to love and be loved. Then your child (or children) in turn can teach their children, and so forth and so on, until the end of time.

The love for a child is humanity in its purest form. Just imagine a world where all life is embraced in that love.

9 798985 408607